FACE TO FACE

Conversations with Voices from the Biblical Narrative

A Series of Monologues from Scripture

By
Rev. David Endriss

Dedication

To my parents, John and Ruby, whose stories are so deeply intertwined with my own: Thank you for teaching me the story.

Reviews for *Face to Face*

❝ Face to Face is a welcome addition to the growing collection of monologues inspired by biblical texts. Created by a thoughtful and experienced pastor, Face to Face includes introductory comments and reflective discussion questions so that clergy and other leaders can easily invite congregation members or study group participants to dialogue about the characters and theological issues the monologues present. Listeners familiar with biblical stories and languages will appreciate humorous references (for example, in the Job monologue H.A. Seytan is the independent counsel), but the monologues will still resonate with listeners who miss some of the subtleties. This intriguing collection combines solid biblical exegesis with creative proclamation.

–Jan Everhart, Ph.D.
Department Chair of Religion
and Associate Professor of
Religion, Simpson College
Ordained Methodist Minister

Reverend Dave's, *Face to Face: Conversations with Voices from the Biblical Narrative*, entices readers to engage in monologues that elevate their understanding of the factual and emotional background of the most powerful biblical stories. By so doing, we realize that we too have shared many of the same struggles, joys, losses and achievements as Job, David, Zacchaeus, Mary, and Paul. We come to better understand the word of

God in our quest to personally interpret God's messages and meaning. While written primarily for pastors who may employ the monologues with their congregation, I found so much meaning and understanding in the narratives that I believe they can be read for personal reflection as well as part of a Bible study class or series. All will benefit from Reverend Dave's years of perfecting stories and storytelling that move us to be proud of our heritage and our struggle to live as Christians.

–Thomas S. Westbrook, Ph.D.
Professor of Leadership Studies,
Drake University

Anyone who thinks the Bible is no more than a curious collection of stories from the faded past with little to commend it to the high tech world of today, think again.

In David Endriss' new book, Face to Face, a parade of characters -- heroes and villains, the famous and the obscure, the wealthy and the impoverished - step out of the biblical past and tell us their stories of God at work in human lives: guiding, loving, and empowering,

A veteran pastor and teacher of the Scriptures, David Endriss has taken selective accounts of biblical characters and retold each one through a dramatic monologue, presented in costume, allowing the audience to hear each story given as a first person account by the character himself. From Job to Jonah, from Zacchaeus to Paul, from David to Peter the personalities and the events in which they played such central roles in God's dealing with man come into the here and now as we meet them face to face.

Providing practical instruction for staging and delivery of each monologue, Face to Face can be used in a wide variety of ministry contexts.

With imagination and vibrant style Endriss has not compromised the message of the Scriptures but given us a potent means to retell the old old story in dramatic fashion tuned into today.

–Rev. John Bristol, retired
Presbyterian Church, U.S.A.

Table of Contents

PREFACE

These pages represent a pilgrimage I have taken through Scripture over the course of many years. I readily confess that the journey is far from over. The stories told in these pages reflect my passion for the biblical story and finding ways to share that story memorably and faithfully.

In the opening pages of this booklet, I intend to share with you something of my personal journey that has helped to shape me into who I am today. I've taken the risk to allow you to take a peek inside my head (perhaps as scary for you as for me) as I share with you the processes that I typically go through in preparing one of these monologues.

The second and largest part of this booklet contains the monologues. Before each monologue, I will share some specifics about the development and challenges of writing and sharing that story. The monologues are listed in the order they appear in our biblical canon, though that is not the order in which they were composed. At the conclusion of each monologue, I have shared some questions that will enable you personally, or in the context of a group discussion, to dig a little deeper into the narrative.

If you find these inspiring and helpful, I am grateful. If you choose to use them in your own worship setting or in the context of a Sunday School class, you have my permission. If they challenge you to write your own monologues taken from the biblical narrative, I am excited for you and your congregations. But most of all, I hope these monologues will lead you back into the story itself: God's wonderful story of grace and love!

To the three congregations I have served (Wasilla Presbyterian Church in Wasilla, AK; First Presbyterian Church in Hallock, MN; Trinity United Presbyterian Church in Indianola, IA):

Thank you for your patience and sensitivity as you have travelled with me on this journey. I am deeply indebted to your faith, your love of God, and how you have ministered to me even as I have sought to minister to you.

Authors often express their gratitude and appreciation to their spouses, whose love, patience and insight has made possible the words they write. And although it may sound trite, like a frequently quoted cliché, it nevertheless remains completely true: without the love of my wife, Nicola, the story of God's love would still exist, but I would have missed the joy of travelling this path with her.

THE MAKING OF A MONOLOGUE

A Word of Power

I find it strange that I may not be able to remember what I had for dinner last night, but to this day I remember when my youth pastor told vividly the story of Gideon from the book of Judges. He made the character come alive. Gideon's fears, his uncertainties, his anxieties, and his victories were shared with drama, humor, and passion. That story has stuck with me for over 40 years, and I too have had the joy of sharing that same story with others.

That's the beautiful thing about the biblical story: from the very beginning, it was meant to be shared. Almost all of the stories in the Bible began as a part of an oral tradition passed verbally from one generation to the next. Eventually, the stories were written down, but they began as stories, like those parents tell their children in the evening before tucking them into bed.

A note to preachers who wish to use the monologue genre in worship: For me, the cardinal sin a preacher can commit is to make the biblical story "boring." And I know I have at times been guilty of that very thing. Woven into the pages of God's word are drama, adventure, romance, comedy, action, and even a little soap opera! (I can't read the story of Jacob, his wives, and his concubines without shaking my head in wonder. "Days of Our Lives" has nothing on Genesis chapters 29-30!)

The biblical narrative has the power to pull you into the story until you become a part of that very story. You ache with Job in his pain, knowing that you too have at times felt lonely and abandoned. You flee with Jonah

3

because there have been times when you know God has wanted you to do one thing but you really wanted to do something else. You repent with Peter, who collapses in tears at the sound of the cock crow, and you know with certainty that, in your own way, you too have denied your Lord.

A Word About Production

The stories listed in this book are told with a simplicity of staging and props. I take a minimalist approach, leaving it to the congregation's imagination to fill in the gaps. Part of this is me being pragmatic; elaborate staging involves time, money, people, and talents that are not always easily accessible. But also, if I may return again to the oral tradition, the early storytellers didn't bring in a donkey when they wanted to tell the story of Balaam's ass in Numbers chapter 22. They told the story with such vividness that you could hear, and perhaps even smell, the animal! They told it in such a way that made you believe the donkey was really there, really talking!

This brings me to one point of tension that inevitably arises when I share one of these monologues on a Sunday morning. I caution you that this should never become a performance; it is rather an expression of worship. If it is in any way a performance, it should have an audience of one: God. "Monologues must never become a 'show' but create the opportunity for genuine worship."[1]

---

[1] Calvin Metcalf, *Voices from the Bible: Dramatic Monologs in Worship* (Colorado Springs, CO: Meriwether Publishing Ltd., 1990), 4.

In the secular world, a performance is understood to take place when one or more people are on a stage entertaining us—the audience—who remain passive in our seats. But a congregation of worshippers should never be passive. If a good story is drawing them into itself, then they are anything but passive. Next time you are listening to a good story-teller, take your eyes off of them (if you can) and look at others who are listening. My guess is that they will be on the edge of their seats, leaning in, captivated by what they are hearing and seeing.

A Word About Preparation

While this is not a performance, it is a service that you offer to God and to the congregation you hope to inspire. Therefore, take seriously the work necessary to do it well. At most, I do only one or two monologues a year with my congregation, and every time I do, it takes a lot out of me. I'm sure those who write monologues have many different methods of developing them. Allow me the privilege to share with you my typical approach.

As you immerse yourself in God's Word, you may discover certain characters and stories that jump out and captivate your imagination. When they do, read, re-read, and read again their stories. Become so familiar with the story that you can easily retell it to another person.

Then, do some research. Study the time and culture of that character. What did suffering from leprosy mean for people in the first century? What were the Assyrians like when Jonah was alive? What was it like to be a chief tax collector in Jericho during the first century?

5

THE MAKING OF A MONOLOGUE

Why was Peter so appalled at God's invitation to eat and drink in his vision on the rooftop in Acts 10? Without some understanding of these issues, your retelling will lack integrity and believability.

Look at commentaries. Study what other scholars have written about the meaning of the story and what kind of an impact its telling over the years has had on the church. This will provide you with valuable material as you begin writing.

As you study these resources, use what the author Randy Alcorn has called "a Scripture-enhanced imagination."[2] Without departing from the text, imagine what is happening to your character in the story. How are they feeling? How are they reacting to the events taking place around them? Imagine their physical movements. How do they interact with their environment? How does your character respond to those who are listening, to other characters in the story, to God, or even to him or herself?

As you begin to write, visualize how your character will move as he or she tells the story to the audience. Then, beyond just physical movements, how is your character feeling and how is he or she expressing those feelings? As you read the stories in this book, you will find some of my suggested movements and emotions written in *italics*.

Then, start writing! And re-writing. And re-re-writing. Speak the words out loud; give them life and breath! You will know when it is right or when it needs to be changed. You will notice in the following

[2] Randy Alcorn, *Heaven* (Wheaton, IL: Tyndale House Publishing, 2004), 21.

monologues that I have often quoted verses straight from the scriptural texts in ways that I believe are faithful to the narrative. Unless otherwise noted, all scripture references are taken from the New Revised Standard Version.

As you write, you will discover the props you need and the blocking of your movements. And then, of course, take the time to practice, practice, and practice until you can tell the story without notes. Someone who reads a monologue from notes immediately puts their listeners at a disadvantage. If you, in character, don't remember your own thoughts, how can you expect others to be drawn into your story? It takes a lot of work, but trust me: it will be worth it!

Be Brave!

Don't be afraid to return to that oral tradition as long as you remain faithful to the story you have received. There is power in the telling! I believe a well-told story needs little interpretation. Most people will "get it"! But even if they don't, they will remember the tale, and I trust that God will help them apply it when the time is right.

BALAAM'S ASS

This monologue was one of the more playful stories I have shared with my congregation over the years. Having already written several monologues, I wanted to try something a little different. I had no staging for this monologue. My only interaction was with the congregation.

In retrospect, choosing this particular character was problematic; at least one author suggests that choosing non-human characters is ill advised because it makes the situation less believable for the congregation.[3] But since the donkey in this story is *supposed* to be talking, I determined it worth a try.

A theme in this story is that God often speaks to us in surprising and unexpected ways. Balaam certainly didn't expect God to speak to him through his donkey! I was willing to "make an ass" of myself if it helped the congregation hear this story in a new way.

---

[3] Stephen Chapin Garner, *Getting into Character; the art of First-Person Narrative Preaching* (Grand Rapids, MI: Brazos Press 2008), 41.

9

PIN THE TAIL ON WHO????

It really isn't fair! I've been around for thousands of years and have been a noble beast of burden to humans for all that time. For the most part, I'm easy going, and although I may not be fast, I can go for a long time. I can be tenacious and very loyal. Be nice to me, and I'll work hard for you! I'm a nice guy! You can usually even perceive a smile on my face. But then some scientist gave me a fancy name, *Equus africanus asinus*, and I have been the butt of jokes ever since (no pun intended!), particularly in America! Oh, and by the way, who came up with that sick game, "Pin the tail on the donkey"? That is simply uncivilized!

Sadly, we are a poorly understood species. We are often called stupid, dumb, or slow. But someone who knows better once wrote, *"Donkeys possess the affectionate nature of a Newfoundland dog, the resignation of a cow, the durability of a mule, the courage of a tiger, and the intellectual capability only slightly inferior to man's."[4]*

And we have a long and sacred history. Owning a significant number of us was a sign of wealth in Old Testament time. Originally, riding into town on one of us showed your affluence. Most people had to walk! We were the BMW's of our day! Later, as the aristocracy started riding those uppity horses, then the opposite became true, and riding into town on us reflected one's humility. Of course, perhaps the most famous member of my family was the one privileged to

---

[4]Robert Green, cited in http://en.wikipedia.org/wiki/Donkey.

give the Messiah a ride into Jerusalem on Palm Sunday. Tradition has it that the Messiah's mother rode to Bethlehem on a donkey when she was pregnant. But believe me: as much as I think the story is cute, I have very little in common with Eeyore from *Winnie-the-Pooh* and even less with the little boys who were turned into donkeys because of their disobedience in the story of *Pinocchio*! I find that offensive, in fact! Nor do we prattle on endlessly like that characterization in the movie "Shrek"! Please don't judge us all by those stories!

But what I really wanted to share with you today is one particular story that illustrates very well how we as a breed have sometimes been taken for granted. It comes from the Old Testament book of Numbers.

My owner, Balaam was a prophet. The Israelites, who were in the process of leaving the desert they had wandered in for forty years, were headed to the land just west of Moab. But in order to get there they had to travel through my country, Moab. It made our king very nervous to have such a large mass of people going through his territory. So the king sent messengers to my master, Baalam, asking that he curse the Israelites.

When the messengers first asked, Balaam prayed and God told him that instead of cursing the Israelites, he should bless them. Needless to say, this did not make the king of Moab very happy, so he sent more servants and more money to my master, again asking him to curse the Israelites. Perhaps the extra money tempted him, because this time, Balaam chose to return with the messengers to see the king.

This is where the story gets interesting. Of course, I was his mode of transportation. Oh, by the way, along with our many other wonderful traits, we are known for being rather perceptive animals, as you shall see. Of course, God was not pleased that my master had chosen to go to the king. So God sent an angel with a sword to prevent us from continuing on the path. Having a rather strong sense of self-preservation, I steered off the path and into a field to avoid the angel. Balaam, not being nearly as perceptive as I, had not seen the angel, so he beat me for getting off the path.

But the angel was not yet done. Now he moved in front of me on the small path in the field so that I was forced up against a wall. Again, Balaam beat me with his stick. But the angel was still not done. This time, he took his stance directly in front of me and there was nowhere for me to go. So I did what my kind have often done for years when we refuse to go further: I sat down! This, of course, really aroused my master to anger, and he struck me again!

Well, God, who had opened my eyes to see the angel in the first place, now opened my mouth so I could talk to my master. Unsurprisingly, the first thing out of my mouth was a complaint, "What have I done to you that you have struck me these three times?"[5]

Now talking donkeys are not an everyday sight, even in the Bible! You would have thought that would be enough of a shock to silence Balaam, but in his anger, he replied, "Because you have failed to take me where I have directed you! You are making a fool of me! If I had a sword, I would kill you!"[6]

---

[5] Numbers 22:28ff
[6] Numbers 22:29.

At that comment, I couldn't help but look at the closest sword at hand: the one the angel was holding. Little did my master know that the sword he wanted to strike me with was poised to strike him!

We donkeys are really sensible, even logical animals. I tried to appeal to his reason. "Am I not your donkey, whom you have ridden all your life? Up to this time, have I ever led you astray?" Quite correctly, Balaam replied, "No."[7]

Finally, along with opening my mouth, God opened my master's eyes to see the same angel I saw. Seeing the angel, Balaam fell to the ground, and the angel said to him, "If it wasn't for your donkey I would have killed you and spared the animal because your way was contrary to God's."[8]

I would have thought that after all these years, I had earned some trust from Balaam. Under normal conditions I am very content to let someone else lead me. Generally speaking, I am a follower. But when the need arises, I can take the reins...again, pardon the pun! When our way is contrary to God's, perhaps we need to learn to trust others, even when it looks like they are taking us off the path we wanted to go on!

My master then confessed his disobedience and his willingness to turn around. Instead, the angel told him to continue on toward the king, seeing as how he was already headed that way. "But," the angel said, "you are to speak to the king only the words that God gives you.[9] And, by the way, God still wants you to bless the Israelites."

---

[7] 22:30.
[8] 22:33.
[9] 22:35.

The rest of the journey, and the story for that matter, was fairly uneventful, at least as it involved me.

I suppose there is some ironic humor to this story: The prophet, the seer of divine things, was the one who was truly blind, and I had more sense and clairvoyance than he did! "I guess if people can speak God's words then why can't that be true of animals?"[10] Or true of anyone else for that matter....even me....even you!

(Exit)

---

[10] Gordon Wenham, *Commentary on Numbers* in Tyndale Commentary Series, Vol 4 (Downers Grove, IL: InterVarsity Press 1981), 121.

Discussion Questions: Balaam's Ass

Consider a time when God has spoken to you from a direction that you did not anticipate. Did God speak through an unexpected event in your life or through an unlikely source?

Has there been a time in your life when it seems that an angel stood firmly in your way to stop you from going down the wrong path and to re-direct you? Describe that experience.

Like Balaam, are there times when we have been so blind and deaf to God's will that we have, even unknowingly, beaten the messenger? Do we need to ask forgiveness both of God and the one God used to speak to us?

To Balaam's credit, he eventually admits to his disobedience and obeys the voice of God. What is the relationship between confession and obedience?

DAVID AND BATHSHEBA

This monologue grew out of a sermon series on the life of David. One commentator, in her opening comments on this sorry story from David's life, said that the *"account of what happened is brief and objective."*[11] This fired up my imagination to tell the story from the perspective of a reporter. Thus, this monologue, unlike the others, is not in the voice of the key biblical character.

I again used no staging for this monologue, though I could have used a simple "news desk" to portray the setting. Since even reporters often read from a well prepared script, I was able to keep my notes before me. I adjusted my vocalizations to mimic a classical reporter who is observing and commenting on the facts of the case.

---

[11] Joyce G Baldwin, *Commentary on 1&2 Samuel* in Tyndale Old Testament Commentaries, Vol 8, (Downers Grove, IL: Intervarsity Press 1988) 232, emphasis mine.

DAVID AND BATHSHEBA

Headlines: Jerusalem—Last night, in a stunning admission of guilt, King David acknowledged that he had an "inappropriate relationship" with Bathsheba, the wife of his loyal servant, Uriah the Hittite. This relationship resulted not only in her pregnancy but in the betrayal and murder of Uriah as he fought in the Royal Army during the Ammonite War. David made the confession after it was made clear that his confidant, Nathan T. Prophet, who was subpoenaed by independent counsel H.A. Seytan, would cooperate with the investigation into the affair. It is rumored that Prophet had received inside information from a source in "high places" about David's involvement in the scandal.

"Have mercy on me, O God," a contrite David said in his speech. "Wash me thoroughly from my iniquity, and cleanse me from my sin."

While some believe the sincerity of his plea, many question whether David's confession is just another "song and dance" for his growing collection of Psalms. Temple insiders admit that because of the "immoral" nature of David's actions, they are forced to debate whether his Book of Psalms should even be included in the sacred canon.

Independent Counsel Seytan, rebounding from his failed probe into Job's faith claims, said in a statement today that he feels vindicated by the recent turn of events. Because he is still completing his report into the Bathsheba affair, Seytan declined further comment. But before disappearing in a puff of smoke, he said he intends to "get to the bottom" of the enigmatic claim made by the king last night, during which the king also admitted that he "was born guilty, a sinner when my mother conceived me."[12]

"If the king's been guilty for that long," Seytan said, "I wonder what else he's trying to hide."

Although Seytan's report will not be released for another few weeks, pundits speculate that it may force the king to resign. Legal experts say the Bathsheba affair, with its adultery, murder, and coveting, violate at least three of the Ten Commandments. David's political foes, who have questioned his kingship since his involvement in the mysterious death of Goliath T. Giant, argue that the king was never fit for office.

This investigative reporter has now decided to delve further into this scandalous story to find out not only the "what" of the story but also the "why." What could lead a powerful man like David to use his position to commit this sexual error and then use that same power to cover up his mistakes? Certainly not since Adam and Eve has such a gross sin been so publically bared.

Upon examination of the evidence, it seems that David's first mistake was being in the wrong place at the wrong time. He had no business being in Jerusalem at the time of the act. As king, his job was to lead his army in battle against the Ammonites. But he opted to stay home in Jerusalem. Was this political arrogance, a gross dereliction of duty, or simple laziness? At 50 years old, this aging monarch seems to be going soft. He seems to be only a shadow of the man who once led the people by slaying the Philistine giant and re-uniting a broken nation.

---

[12] Psalm 51:5

It was a warm Jerusalem night when the trouble began. This reporter, although having never been in the king's private quarters himself, has studied blueprints of the building. As one might expect, the king's house is situated in such a way that he can look down upon the entire city. Seeking refuge from the oppressive heat one evening, the king escaped to the coolness of his patio roof. One insider is reported to have heard the king say, "I am master of all I survey."

Then it happened. Peering over his balcony, he saw a beautiful woman, Bathsheba. She was bathing in her courtyard. There are mixed reports regarding whether she was naked or simply washing her feet. The written testimony only says she was bathing. This reporter chooses to believe her innocence because, in the prophet's later condemnations, there is no mention of her wrong-doing. But now begins the king's spiraling downfall.

One servant, who has requested anonymity, reported that the king asked him who that beautiful woman was. The servant responded, she is "Bathsheba, the daughter of Eliam, the wife of Uriah the Hittite." Kudos to this servant, who could see in his master's eyes the fire that didn't belong there. Subtly the servant let the king know that she was unavailable. She was married.

Undeterred, the king ordered that she be brought to him. He then slept with her and sent her back to her house. Later, she sent those fateful words to the king: "I am pregnant." The king was now in a quandary. Palace informants have spoken of David's nervous pacing as he sought for a solution to this conundrum. Bathsheba's husband was off faithfully fighting the Ammonites (as the king should have been doing). With him gone, there would be little doubt as to who fathered the child.

But then the king had an idea. The palace scribe was called to take a letter. This letter was sent to Commander Joab on the front lines of the war requesting that Uriah the Hittite be sent back to Jerusalem to report to the king on the progress of the war and to take a few days of furlough. When Uriah arrived, the king feigned interest in his report, but in reality was only hoping to send him off to his house so that he would sleep with his wife and rid the king of any possible implications.

However, several witnesses, whose testimonies have been corroborated, said that Uriah did not return to his house but chose to sleep at the door of the palace with the rest of the king's servants. Puzzled and frustrated at this, the king asked Uriah why he didn't go home. This reporter cannot help but shake his head at the irony of this situation. Uriah was a Hittite, not even a Jew, but he told the King of Israel what was proper.

Uriah said, *"The ark and Israel and Judah remain in booths; and my lord Joab and the servants of my lord are camping in the open field; shall I then go to my house, to eat and to drink, and to lie with my wife? As you live, and as your soul lives, I will not do such a thing."*[13] Uriah's conscience and integrity as a loyal soldier would not allow him the luxury of hearth and home for even one night while his fellow soldiers were roughing it on the battlefield. Things would have gone far better had the king heard and acted on the advice of

---

[13] 2 Samuel 11:11

this loyal follower. But David was determined to try once again.

Kitchen servants have verified that the next night, the king set before Uriah a wonderful banquet in hopes that if he got sufficiently drunk, he would return to his home and sleep with his wife. But still, the faithful Uriah refused to return to his house.

Frustrated to the point of desperation, the king conceived of a devious, terrible plan. He had another letter written, which this reporter has seen, instructing general Joab to put Uriah in the front of the worst fighting and then to retreat, leaving him alone. This letter was sealed and given to Uriah to deliver to his commander. Tragically unaware, Uriah carried his own death warrant!

You may recall last year's headlines about our surprise defeat in battle with the Ammonites. At that time, military analysts criticized general Joab for leading the army in a foolish plan that ended the lives of many loyal Israelite soldiers. We now see that this plan was not of Joab's doing at all. It was by order of the king himself. At the end of that battle, the general sent a letter back to the king apologizing for the ignominious defeat. The public expected the king to write back a scathing letter of rebuke, perhaps even dismissal. Instead, David's reply amounted to something along the lines of, "Don't worry about it. Fortunes of war and all that." In light of the current events and revelations, we now know why the king responded in such a way, that the defeat was the king's way of getting rid of Uriah.

That was over a year ago. Since he was apparently successful with his cover up, the king married

Bathsheba and the child was born in the palace. This political reporter cannot help but wonder who the king was trying to fool. Between sleeping with Bathsheba and marrying her, several months passed. It has been my observation that most adults are able to count to nine. Who is the king trying to deceive?

The king's cover up seemed so successful that there was no story to investigate until last week when the king's prophet and longtime confidant, Nathan, confronted the monarch. It took a great deal of courage to approach the king. My respect and admiration for Nathan has increased immeasurably.

As a political correspondent, I was in the royal court with the rest of the press corps when the prophet met with the king. It is not uncommon for the monarch to preside over difficult judicial proceedings. It was during the trial over one of these disputes that the prophet confronted the king. Since I was present, I took down his story word for word.

The prophet stated the situation: *"There were two men in a certain city, the one rich and the other poor. The rich man had very many flocks and herds; but the poor man had nothing but one little ewe lamb, which he had bought. He brought it up, and it grew up with him and with his children; it used to eat of his meager fare, and drink from his cup, and lie in his bosom, and it was like a daughter to him. Now there came a traveler to the rich man, and he was loath to take one of his own flock or herd to prepare for the wayfarer who had come to him, but he took the poor man's lamb, and prepared that for the guest who had come to him.* "[14]

---

[14] 2 Samuel 12:1-4

The king's reaction was immediate and harsh. He was incensed!

"That man ought to die!" roared the king.

What Nathan said next brought a shocked silence to the whole court. He declared: "You are that man!"

Never have I seen a man so cleverly and so completely disarmed. With his own words, David condemned himself. He was stunned, his mouth stuck open in utter amazement that his secret was out. And as the prophet continued with his condemnation, the king slid off of his throne and collapsed to his knees.

With tears in his eyes, he confessed, "I have sinned against the Lord."

I have served as a political reporter for more years than I care to count. As such, it has become easy for me to be cynical about politicians and their often cheap words. But I can tell you from first-hand knowledge, there was nothing phony about the king's confession and repentance. The king was truly sorry for his mistakes and perhaps even grateful that he was finally exposed. In this he is different from his predecessor, Saul, who never truly repented from his mistakes.

It is for this very reason that the prophet said to David, "Now the Lord has put away your sin; you shall not die." The prophet made it very clear there would be some major consequences because of his error, but David would survive.

In concluding my investigative report, I would like to make the following personal observations in the form of an editorial. In some ways, the king's sins are no greater than ours—yours and mine—but ours have not been publically bared for all to see. For that I am personally, very grateful. Still, I believe we as a people can learn from the king's mistakes.

The king's first error was that he was not where he was supposed to be in the very beginning of this sorry episode. Had he been diligent in his work out on the battlefield, he would have never been tempted to commit adultery in the first place. Idle hands can indeed be the devil's playground.

Secondly, when temptation did come in the appealing form of Bathsheba bathing, the king would have been wise to flee, to escape off of his patio roof instead of staring. After all, isn't that what Joseph did in Egypt when the wife of Potiphar made a pass at him? Fleeing temptation is about the only way to survive it.

Sin, unconfessed and covered up tends to feed on itself. The king's frantic attempt to hide his sin has now, ironically, become one of the most infamous stories of adultery. One sin led to another, which led to another. But eventually, it caught up with him. It has been said that "God's wheels grind slowly, but they grind exceedingly fine." It would have been so much easier for the king, for Bathsheba, for Uriah, and for the entire nation if David had confessed early on.

But there is hope. If forgiveness and restoration is possible for an adulterer and a murderer who truly repents, certainly there is mercy for anyone who confesses with an open heart. This reporter is only too aware of his own shortcomings and hopes that all will find the courage to confess their sins before God and seek the forgiveness that is then possible—the forgiveness even King David was given.

Discussion Questions: David and Bathsheba

(Note: If these questions are being discussed in a group setting, the facilitator/leader should make it clear that people need share only what they are comfortable sharing.)

Do we sometimes put ourselves in the wrong place, thus unnecessarily opening the door for the possibility of sin to enter our lives? Describe a time in which this has happened to you.

When temptation does occur, what is our response? Do we indulge or flee? Do we stare or do we pray? Joseph is mentioned in the monologue as one example of someone who fled temptation. What other biblical examples can you name of people who avoided temptation? How did they do it?

Consider the relationship between confession, forgiveness and the consequences of sin. While forgiveness cleanses us from guilt, are there still after-effects for which we must take responsibility? Can you suggest some examples?

JOB

Of all the monologues I have written and shared with my congregations, this one, unsurprisingly, took the most out of me emotionally. Playing the role of distraught parent, angry follower of God, self-righteous victim of the divine whims, and betrayed companion of so called friends is not easy!

Job is clothed with an outer robe and a simple inner cloak. The inner cloak is made of coarse cloth with a hole in the middle and is tied at the waist with a rope. The outer robe hangs loosely off the shoulders, untied.

The remains of a campfire and some broken pottery make for a simple stage. The pottery is used to scrape boils, and the ashes are a sign of mourning. At one point in the monologue there is an off stage voice that tempts Job to deny God. Other off stage sounds include the growing sound of wind and the voice of God. Finally, hidden among the remains of the campfire is a small toy spider that reminds Job of God's great creation.

Job is one of those biblical characters and stories that has often puzzled people. Why did this righteous man suffer so much? What were his friends trying to say to him? How is his story relevant today?

But the question of suffering is just as relevant a question today as it was in Job's time. Job's conversation with his friends and with God is a dialogue I wanted to share with my congregation because it is the kind of conversation that we have all had at one time or another.

JOB MONOLOGUE

(Job enters, sits on the floor near a burned out fire, covers his head in prayerful meditation, and gently begins rocking back and forth. After a few moments he notices visitors...)

It may seem odd to you, but I return to this place often. It helps me to keep things in perspective. I guess we probably all need a place like this. If we don't have one, we should find one. Why is this place so special to me? After all, it doesn't look like much. The scenery is not too spectacular. A burned out campfire...it doesn't even have decent chairs! This place is special for me because it was here that I spent several weeks wrestling with myself, my friends, and even my God.

My story? It actually begins much sooner than this place. *(Smiling, he is thinking back to that time. He stands.)* When I was younger I enjoyed a fair amount of success—success by just about anyone's standards. I had a loving and caring wife. I had a small herd of adoring children who were healthy and, for the most part, responsible. I was wealthy. *(He makes an expansive gesture.)* I had fields covered with livestock of all kinds and I employed the many necessary hands to take care of them. I was easily one of the wealthiest men in the region.

But success also came in other ways. People came to me for advice. Sometimes it was financial. They thought I knew something about business. But often it was about other things: family, theology, even their personal problems. I guess people thought I might have had the answers they wanted.

28

All these forms of success are good, but I found my greatest satisfaction in knowing God. Oh, don't misunderstand me, I don't think of myself as a spiritual giant like Moses or Abraham. I just found great personal fulfillment in knowing God and knowing that God knew me.

Then, one day, all of this changed quite suddenly. Within a short hour, my children were killed in a building accident and my livestock were either killed in a violent storm or stolen by a raiding band of thieves. Along with my children and my livestock, many of my servants were killed!

This news tore at my heart *(He tears his robe and throws to the side).* It was one brutal blow after another. *(He beats his breast.)* It quite literally knocked me to the ground. *(He returns to the ground near the campfire.)* It seemed so terribly unfair. And yet *(he looks at his partially naked self),* "naked I came from my mother's womb into this world, and naked I will depart. The Lord gave and the Lord has taken away; may the name of the Lord be praised."[15]

Does that sound too flippant? Or maybe even uncaring and insensitive? After all, I had just lost almost everything that I had! Oh, trust me, it hurt. But I had not given up on God. But if I thought things couldn't possibly get worse…

Not long after, I developed a skin disease. Big ugly sores and boils appeared all over my body. They festered and oozed to such an extent that I took a broken piece of pottery *(picking up a piece of pottery)* and used it to scrape off the worst places.

---

[15] Job 1:21 (New International Version)

(He draws attention to the ashes in fire and picks up a handful.) Ashes to ashes, dust to dust. This is what I am and it is to this that I shall return. Little wonder that ashes are a sign of death and mourning. *(He begins spreading ashes on the exposed areas of flesh.)* But the final straw, the final stab of the knife came when my own wife advised me to reject God...to curse him and die!

I had lost it all: my children, my possessions, even my health. Now, in hindsight, I guess I can truly say I hadn't lost everything. I still had a few friends. In the past I had helped them through difficult times; now it was their turn to help me. There was Eliphaz, Bildad, and Zophar. They had heard of my troubles and dropped everything to come to me.

How I had fallen in their eyes! No longer was I the image of prosperity and happiness. I went from regal robes and a healthy complexion to rags and scabs. I can't blame them for not recognizing me at first! I didn't recognize myself!

As good friends, they did nothing at first. They sat and cried with me. They listened to my agonized groans. They suffered with me as I sought to scrape away not only the boils but the layers of disasters that had fallen upon me. *(He scrapes vigorously with a potsherd.)* But it was no use. The potsherd was not big enough. It could not cut deep enough to rid myself of my pain. I needed something else *(he discards the potsherd)* I needed to find relief from my suffering...

(With anguish, anger, suffering, and accusation, he says) GOD!!! No more. No more. I wish that I had never been born. What was the purpose of it all if it must end like this? Why has God put me through this?

If this is life, then why live? *(With a sigh and great weariness, he says)* I can't fight it any more. I've been attacked on all sides. There is no place for me to hide in order to find peace.

Even my sleep brought no respite. I tossed and turned. Shadows and evil specters lurked in my nightmares, teasing me with their seductive charm. *(The offstage voice or tape begins to play.)* "What kind of God do you worship? Some believer you are! Cast aside your faith; it is as useless as that potsherd!" *(Pause)*

(Standing, he says) Well, even good friends can only take so much. After listening to my ranting and raving for seven days, they felt compelled to answer some of my questions. Funny how some people want to try and answer questions that were not even addressed to them! I was talking, no *screaming*, to God! But I guess they felt that they had God's answers!

Sympathetically, and ever so gently, they tried to soothe my troubled spirit. "Uhh, Job, I know this has been tough on you, but if you can patiently listen for a few moments, I have some thoughts that I would like to share".

Do me a favor, will you? When someone is in terrible pain and suffering, as their friend, don't get into a theological argument with them. I needed a hospital; they gave me a seminary. I wanted, no I *needed*, to vent my frustration and confusion.

I guess when we see great pain and suffering, we either run away from it or we want to fix it and make it all better. But these friends couldn't do that with their words. Oh, but they tried! Oh, did they try! If words were bandages, I would have been mummified many

times over by their words. So many words...so little
salve to ease the pain of my heart...

Still, they tried. At first it was gentle and easy.
Their point was fairly straightforward. It went
something like this: Once life was good to you, Job.
Obviously, God was happy with you. Now things are
bad. God is unhappy with you. Somewhere in the
middle, you did something that made God unhappy.
Confess your mistake to God and things will get back to
normal once again.

Sounds pretty good, doesn't it? If only it was that
easy. There was one little problem with their idea: For
the life of me, I couldn't think of anything that I had
done wrong! Oh, that's not to say I'm perfect—who is
in the eyes of God? But I hadn't changed my way of
behaving. I had done nothing different that would have
precipitated this calamity.

My friends and I argued back and forth at great
length about this. They began to insist that I was in
denial and that my defiance in itself was a part of my
rebellion against God. The more I stubbornly refused to
grant them their point, the more insistent they became.

I once heard it said that my life has become a source
of proverbially wisdom. Some even wished that they
had the "patience of Job." Ha! Those people obviously
hadn't talked with my three friends! I wanted answers
from God, and I wanted them NOW! Patience? I think
not.

Eventually, it came to the point where, to justify
their position, they argued that because of my obstinate
attitude, I hadn't been punished enough! *(He smiles a
wry smile.)* With friends like that...

Oh, there was one other friend who was present. Elihu. He had been quiet for all this time. Despite his younger age, he showed much greater wisdom than the others. The others had finally thrown up their hands in frustration with me. I think they had finally given up trying to convince me of the errors of my ways. It was only then that Elihu ventured to speak. At first he laid into the others who so callously tore into me. He told them that they had missed the mark. Then he sought permission from me to share his thoughts.

That Elihu. *(He smiles.)* He is some preacher! With great eloquence, he said the real question is not about whether I've done something right or wrong. It's simply a question about who is in control: Job or God? The other three and I had been working under what we thought was a universal and unchanging truth. The righteous are blessed by God and live fruitful lives. The wicked are punished. The corollary is that if you are suffering, then God must be punishing you, and you therefore must be wicked. The other three thought the problem rested with me. I thought the problem rested with God. Elihu reminded me that we were all functioning under a false premise. The reality is that righteous people sometimes suffer by no particular fault of their own.

His thoughts were like a fresh wind that blew new ideas into my head. *(The offstage wind sound begins and increases.)* And the wind blew harder and harder until it was no longer Elihu speaking: it was God. In the whirlwind, God's voice spoke and challenged me. *(The offstage voice or tape—dubbed over wind—begins.)* "Where were you, Job, when I created the universe? Were you there when I planted the stars into the sky and forged the mountains? Were you there when I separated the night and the day?

"Do you know all the details about the animals I created? Do you know the miracle of how they give birth? Speak Job! Tell me that you know about the mountain goats and the lions. Speak to me of the wild donkey, the ostrich, and the horse. Or what about the great beasts, behemoth or the leviathan? Their great strength causes even the bravest to tremble. Tell me that you understand these things Job."[16] *(The wind fades out.)*

With every line that God spoke, I shrank in recognition that I had spoken out of turn. I had dared to impugn that God was out of line! "Surely I spoke of things I did not understand, things too wonderful for me to know. Therefore, I despise myself and repent in dust and ashes."[17] *(He sits back down among the ashes of the fire.)*

God heard my prayer and forgave my pride. I even had to pray for my wayward friends who had misrepresented God!

Yes, I do like to return to this place often. It helps me remember my place in God's great scheme of things. *(He finds and picks up a spider in and among the wood of the fire.)* And in the world around me, I see God's greatness and I am full of wonder once again.

I suppose in a sense my question was never really answered. My question is one that I suspect we all struggle with from time to time: Why do bad things happen to good people? I guess it's a good question, but

---

[16] Selected verses from Job chapters 38-41
[17] Job 42:3,6

I no longer worry about it. I can live with the bad, if I know that God has not forgotten me. That God is still present. That God is still in control. That God still loves and cares.

I can live with not knowing the "whys" and "wherefores" of suffering. It remains a mystery. But then, there are a lot of mysteries I don't understand about God. *(He studies the spider closely.)* It's enough for me that God understands. *(He carefully places spider back among the wood and stands up.)* Yes, this place has become sacred to me, not as a place to remember my past miseries but as a place where God continues to remind me that it is God, not Job, who remains in control.

(Exit)

Discussion Questions: Job

Can you identify a time when you believe you have suffered unfairly? How did that feel?

Put yourself in the place of one of Job's friends. What would you have done or said? What should be done or said? How might you apply these ideas the next time you visit someone in the hospital or meet with a grieving friend?

At the end of the monologue, God speaks of the wonders of creation. How does the omnipotence of God help Job? Does it solve the riddle of why suffering happens to the righteous?

How comfortable are you with mystery? Does faith need to have all the answers?

JONAH

The story of Jonah is such a familiar one that I wanted to tell it in its entirety, showing the interior conflict that this prophet had with God. Jonah's nationalistic bias has a great deal to say to our world today and to believers who dare to presume upon whom God cares to save.

This monologue is unique among those I have done because it required some onstage assistants to help with props and the action. Although there are no lines for them, their role was crucial. I enlisted the help of a couple of high school students who took great joy in throwing a cup of water in their pastor's face!

The opening scene depicts the prophet very comfortable and at ease. With a patio chair and lemonade in hand, Jonah is very content. A folded map is nearby. He is content in this place until a messenger (someone dressed as a FedEx employee with an official looking envelope) arrives with a package and then leaves. This role is repeated three times during the story.

During the scene on the ocean, a large blue sheet is carried by two aides. With one hand they hold the sheet, and with the other hand (hidden from the congregation) one assistant holds a cup of water and the other holds a strand of seaweed. When the storm hits, they shake the sheet vigorously, indicating waves.

When Jonah jumps into the ocean and is hit by the cup of water, the aides wrap Jonah in the sheet and the aide with the seaweed drapes it on his shoulders. This represents Jonah in the belly of the great fish. If possible, the lights could dim at this scene. The entire prayer of Jonah in the belly of the fish is done while he is wrapped in the blue sheet. To show Jonah being spewed out, the aides quickly spin the sheet, freeing Jonah and revealing the strand of seaweed.

After Jonah preaches in Nineveh, he retreats to see what will happen. A large parasol or umbrella serves as the shade tree. A bright lamp can serve as the sun. An aide can "plant" the tree, make it "wilt," and then turn on the sun.

JONAH THE RELUCTANT DISCIPLE

(Opening: Jonah enters, sits comfortably in an outdoor patio chair, and begins sipping lemonade.)

Ahh, this is the life! Things are going really well. I have the ear of King Jeroboam. He listens to what I say and trusts me. And because of that, I am honored by others at court. Yes, the life of a successful prophet is a good life. I could get used to this!

(Enter: Fed-Ex employee with envelope. He or she hands it to Jonah, gets his signature, and exits.)

What's this? Addressed to Jonah, the prophet, the son of Amittai: that's me. But the return address is a little obscure: "Closer than you think." I wonder who that might be?

(Jonah opens the envelope and reads.)

"Go at once to Nineveh, that great city, and cry out against it; for their wickedness has come up before me."[18] Oh, it's from you. *(He looks to heaven.)* But to Nineveh? Nineveh! You know where that is God? Of course you do. But they are Israel's sworn enemy! Of course they're wicked! They are the bad guys! Why do you want me to go there? It would be a wasted trip. You want me to preach to them? Just send them to Hell! That's where they belong! Nineveh is over 400 miles away! But I wouldn't preach to them even if they

―――――――――――――

[18] Jonah 1:2

39

were next door! They deserve everything that's coming to them.

No way am I going to Nineveh. In fact, I think it's time for a vacation. Let's see... *(He reaches for map.)* Nineveh is east, so I am headed to the west. Let's see, Tarshish seems a good candidate. It's well over two thousand miles in the opposite direction. That should serve me very nicely.

(He walks down aisle of sanctuary and around room while the blue sheet is brought to front by assistants dressed in black, one assistant has a cup of water, the other a string of seaweed—both hidden.)

Ahh, nothing like an ocean voyage to purge the mind of unwanted thoughts! I'll just pay my fare, and settle down for a nap. *(He lies down on a level that is above water line. After a few seconds the water begins to move, becoming progressively more agitated until it finally awakens Jonah who yawns, stretches, and becomes alarmed.)*

What's going on? We are in a storm! I should have known better than to try and run away from God. Truly there is no place where I could flee from God's presence! It's not fair to the crew of this ship that they should drown for my disobedience. There can be only one solution. I must give myself up to God and the ocean. *(He jumps off the top step and into the blue sheet. An assistant with cup of water throws it into Jonah's face, who sputters. Then the blue sheet is wrapped around Jonah, hiding him from the congregation. The assistant with the seaweed drapes it upon Jonah.)*

"In trouble, deep trouble, I prayed to God. He answered me.

From the belly of the grave I cried, 'Help!' You heard my cry.

You threw me into ocean's depths, into a watery grave,

With ocean waves, ocean breakers crashing over me.

I said, 'I've been thrown away, thrown out, out of your sight.

I'll never again lay eyes on your Holy Temple.'

Ocean gripped me by the throat. The ancient Abyss grabbed me and held tight.

My head was all tangled in seaweed at the bottom of the sea where the mountains take root. I was as far down as a body can go, and the gates were slamming shut behind me forever— Yet you pulled me up from that grave alive, O God, my God!

When my life was slipping away, I remembered God,

And my prayer got through to you, made it all the way to your Holy Temple.

Those who worship hollow gods, god-frauds, walk away from their only true love.

But I'm worshiping you, God, calling out in thanksgiving!

And I'll do what I promised I'd do! Salvation belongs to God!"[19]

---

[19] Jonah 2:2-9 (The Message)

(The blue sheet unwinds rapidly, spitting Jonah out onto land. Jonah has seaweed wrapped around his neck and head. The assistants exit with sheet.)

Ewwwww! *(He removes the seaweed)* Thanks a lot, God.

(As Jonah cleans himself off, a Fed-Ex employee enters with another letter. Jonah signs. Fed-Ex exits.)

What? Another letter. Let me guess who this is from. *(He opens the envelope and reads.)* "Get up, go to Nineveh, that great city, and proclaim to it the message that I tell you." (*He looks to God.*) What is this, a Xerox copy of your last letter? Okay, okay, I get the message. Obviously, there is no getting out of this one!

(Jonah begins the journey, wandering through congregation proclaiming...)

"Forty days more, and Nineveh shall be over-thrown!"[20] Repent you heathen barbarians! God has seen your wickedness and has declared an end to your days!

(Finding his way back to the front, Jonah now examines the "city.")

I don't believe it! They are actually repenting! I knew this would happen! *(Accusing God...)* They didn't

---

[20] Jonah 3:4

deserve your mercy, but *noooo*, I know you. The second they show any sign of contrition, you are all too ready to forgive. It's not fair! Besides, I just spent my time going through that city proclaiming its divine destruction. Now you are going to change your mind?! Do you know how that makes me look? So much for being a successful prophet. No one will ever believe me again! I've had it! That's it. I'm moving out of the city. Perhaps you will just change your mind again and destroy the city. I'm going to sit over here and watch.

(An assistant comes out with large umbrella/parasol and provides shade from above and behind Jonah)

Boy, on this hot day, I'm sure glad I found this tree to make me comfortable. *(With glee, he says,)* Those poor souls will just have to suffer. *(The umbrella starts to fold and wither.)* Hey! Where is my shade? Nooo! Some nasty old worm is killing off my tree! *(The umbrella is now replaced with high intensity lamp shining down on Jonah.)* It's just not fair! First, you try and drown me, and now you are going to fry me! God, what are you doing to me?!

(Another Fed-Ex assistant enters with a third envelope; Jonah signs and Fed-Ex exits.) Hmmm, I didn't really expect an answer so promptly! *(He opens the envelope and reads.)*

"Jonah, how is it that you can change your feelings from pleasure to anger overnight about a mere shade tree that you did nothing to get? You neither planted nor watered it. It grew up one night and died the next night. So why can't I likewise change what I feel about Nineveh, from anger to pleasure—this big city of more than a hundred and twenty thousand childlike people who don't yet know right from wrong, to say nothing of all the innocent animals?"[21]

(Jonah, properly chastised, kneels in prayer and then exits.)

---

[21] Jonah 4:10-11 (The Message)

Discussion Questions: Jonah

Who are *our* Ninevites or Assyrians? Who do we know who are so diametrically opposed to our political, ideological, theological, or cultural point of view that we may feel toward them what Jonah felt toward the Ninevites?

Jonah has been called the reluctant disciple. In what ways have we been reluctant disciples?

Has God ever needed to use a big fish to swallow you in order to get your attention?

Even after arriving in Nineveh, Jonah was hardly a gracious messenger. He preached judgment with the possibility of forgiveness that he didn't really want them to have. God can and does use Jonah even when Jonah wished that God would have left things alone. Is there a time when God used you even when you fought against it?

THE PRODIGAL SONS

Along with the story of the Good Samaritan, this parable is one of the most familiar and can easily be repeated by many long-time church goers. But as several commentators have suggested, the real prodigal in this story may not be the younger son. It may in fact be the older one—the son who never left home. All of the "Lost Parables" that Jesus told in Luke chapter 15 were initiated by the Pharisees' complaints that Jesus welcomed sinners and ate with them.

In telling this story, I wanted to do it from the perspective and in the person of the older son, whose frustration and anger with both his younger brother and with the father are palpable.

The staging consists of a simple table in the middle with a chair. On the table are some papers and coins. Off stage on one side is a road to the house where the father is longingly looking for his younger son's return. Off stage on the same side and closer is the location of the party deeper inside the house. On the far side of the stage is where the older son retreats when he rejects his father's invitation. Before each of the closing scenes, I have the voice of the father (from offstage) making the offer to come inside with the rest of the guests. The older son is also wearing a signet ring.

At the end of the parable, Jesus used a literary and rhetorical device that leaves his audience wondering. The father invites the older brother into the celebration, but we are not told if he accepts that invitation. Did he remain outside or did he go into the house? Jesus does not tell us.

THE PRODIGAL SONS: *Luke 15:11-32*

Toward the end of this monologue, I reenact the closing scene twice: once where he refuses the invitation, and again in which he accepts the invitation and goes with his father into the house.

THE PRODIGAL SONS MONOLOGUE

(The son is sitting at the desk and gesturing to his imagined father, who is looking down the road.) There he stands, waiting, waiting, waiting. Doesn't he have anything better to do? There are servants to command, household tasks to oversee, and finances to manage. What is he waiting for? He's not going to return—that younger son of his. I don't want to even admit that he is my brother. We are so different. I'm responsible; he's rash. I'm forward thinking; he lives for the moment. I'm loyal; he's fickle. I work hard; he hardly works. It's difficult for me to believe that we come from the same parents.

This all began months ago when that little brat suddenly announced that he wanted his rightful inheritance now rather than waiting until Dad died. What a hurtful slap in the face that was! He basically told Dad that he wished he was dead! But just as shocking as the request was that Dad actually gave him the money! Didn't Dad know what he was going to do with it? Oh, I knew! He was going to spend it on loose living, women, parties, carousing, and drinking. There would be late night orgies, fancy clothes, and cheap friends purchased at the cost of a beer.

What was the boy thinking? Does he think money grows on trees? Does he think there is a never ending supply? Dad's rich, but his share of the inheritance needed to be invested, not squandered. Frankly, I'm not sure who is more culpable: the brat for asking or Dad for actually giving it to him.

That was months ago, and still he waits. He stands at the door or looks out the window, his eyes focused several hundred yards down the road and his mind absorbed with thoughts of his wayward son. Every time he sees someone on the road he jumps up only to be all the more disappointed when it isn't him.

Look! It's happening again! Dad, relax. You are going to give yourself a coronary! You are only going to be disappointed all over again. But no, not this time. My father's sharp eyes have seen what I did not. It is him! Ahhh, no wonder I didn't recognize him! He left months ago cocky, self-assured, dressed to impress, and strutting like a peacock! (*With glee he says,*) Not now! This young man is dressed in rags, emaciated, feet shuffling, and head bowed with the weight of guilt and shame upon him. I should think so! He certainly got his just deserts!

Dad, what are you doing!? Come back here! You shouldn't be running! It's undignified! It's disgraceful! It's, it's...embarrassing! What will the neighbors think? (*Louder now, he says,*) What's that? I didn't hear what you said. You don't care what the neighbors think? (*To himself he says,*) You don't care? You don't care! You shouldn't be running to him! You should be standing here at the door and letting him come to you. He should be the one groveling on his hands and knees before you.

Well, this ought to be an interesting reunion! Dad is in good shape and even in a robe he is covering the distance in no time. As he approaches, he raises his hands. I'm sure he will grab that prodigal by the throat and strangle him. (*He mimes the action.*) He certainly deserves a good throttling!

But no, those same arms embrace instead of strangle. Even from here, I can hear his tears of joy instead of anger. The boy drops to his knees before father and begins his well-rehearsed speech: "Father, I've sinned against God, I've sinned before you; I don't deserve to be called your son ever again."[22] But Dad isn't having any of it. He hauls him back to his feet without ever letting go of him. With one arm around his shoulders, Father begins issuing commands to nearby servants, who rush off in different directions. One dashes into the house to get fresh clothes and the family signet ring *(He shows the audience his own ring)*, which he obviously lost or pawned for more beer money. He discarded his ring as thoughtlessly as he rejected this family! Dad shouts another order, and a different servant takes off to the corral to pick out the choicest calf for a special dinner. A third servant is instructed to run into town and let everyone know that this prodigal has returned. There is going to be a party tonight and all are invited! Well, I'm not sure I'm coming! *(He stomps off to one side of stage.)*

Just listen to that music! What kind of father throws a party for a son who rejected his family, told his father he would just as soon see him dead, and then squandered the family inheritance on immoral living?! You are not supposed to reward that kind of behavior with a celebration! Where's the justice in that?

(He realizes Dad has come to bring him to the party.) Dad, this is outrageous! "Look how many years I've stayed here serving you, never giving you one moment of grief, but have you ever thrown a party for me and my friends? Then this son of yours who has thrown away your money on whores shows up and you

---

[22] Luke 15:21 (The Message)

go all out with a feast!"[23] *(He pauses with his back to the congregation.)*

Ending One: Older Brother Stays Away

(An off stage voice says,) "Son, you don't understand. You're with me all the time, and everything that is mine is yours—but this is a wonderful time, and we had to celebrate. This brother of yours was dead, and he's alive! He was lost, and he's found!"[24]

(Performer turns and faces the congregation, addressing them.) Jesus' story ends abruptly right there. It forces me to wonder: did the older son remain on the outside or did he come into the house and into the party? The younger son who was the prodigal is now home, but is the older son now the real prodigal? I wonder... *(Performer turns again away from the congregation and pauses a few seconds before turning around again and beginning.)*

For years I have been offended with the behavior of that younger son of my father. *(With a sneer he says,)* He has Daddy wrapped around his little finger. He can do anything and get away with it! But as disgusting as his actions are, I am even more revolted by my Father's. How dare he spread his love and forgiveness around as lavishly as he does his money! He may welcome him back, but he is no brother of mine!

---

[23] Luke 15:29-30 (The Message)
[24] Luke 15:31-32 (The Message)

And if he is no brother of mine, then maybe I am no son of his. *(He takes off the signet ring, slams it on the table, and turns his back to congregation.)*

Ending Two: Older Brother Joins in the Party

(An off stage voice says,) "Son, you don't understand. You're with me all the time, and everything that is mine is yours—but this is a wonderful time, and we had to celebrate. This brother of yours was dead, and he's alive! He was lost, and he's found!"

(He turns toward the imagined father and party off stage.) You are with me. I think I understand. When you were staring out that window, you were not simply waiting; you were with him, even there, in his parties, in his pig sty. And when you could be in the party with my brother, you chose to be here with me. You are with me...but I have not been with you!

(He drops to his knees.) "Father, I've sinned against God, I've sinned before you; I don't deserve to be called your son ever again."

But like he did for my brother, Dad would have none of it. He hauls me to my feet *(He stands)*, places his arm around me, and escorts me into the house. And on the way out, he hands me the family ring *(He picks it up, admires it, and places it on his finger)*. Yes, everything that is his is mine. On this day, two prodigals have returned home.

(Exit)

THE PRODIGAL SONS: *Luke 15:11-32*

Discussion Questions: The Prodigal Sons

Read through the story again from Luke 15 and write down the different emotions you imagine the older brother having at each part of the story. Is there one in particular that resonates with you?

Many of Jesus' parables, particularly in Matthew, begin with, "The Kingdom of God is like..." This parable suggests that God's kingdom is like a family. In what ways is this true?

Jesus seems to purposely leave us hanging as to whether the older son accepts his father's invitation to enter into the party. Why do you think Jesus did that?

How do you think the older son responded? Did he reject the invitation, or did he enter into the house? Why?

THE GRATEFUL LEPER

I wanted to write a monologue telling one of the healing miracles of Jesus. I chose the story of the one leper out of the ten healed by Jesus who returned to express his gratitude. It was one of the first monologues I wrote, and in it I wanted to express the horrific physical, social, spiritual, and relational stigmas associated with leprosy and the profound gratitude expressed by the one leper who returned. I originally shared this monologue with my congregation on the Sunday prior to Thanksgiving.

For this character, a simple rag robe works well. When describing the physical effects of leprosy, I pull my hands into the folds of the robe, indicating not just the physical degeneration of the body but also the immense shame that comes with it.

Gratitude is itself a form and expression of healing, but this story cautions us to remember that the other nine Jews were also healed. Only those who we would expect to be the religiously informed in this story missed out on the healing power of gratitude. It was the Samaritan, the foreigner, who was made whole in fullest measure.

A VOICE OF THANKSGIVING

UNCLEAN! UNCLEAN! There is a leper in your midst! Be warned! Stay back! According to Levitical law, you must stay away or you too shall become unclean! Those were the words I had to say so often before. You see, I was a leper. What is leprosy, you ask? In your time, I understand it is called Hanson's disease, and you are fortunate enough to have medicines that curb its disastrous effects. But in my time, leprosy was considered a terrible curse. In its worst form, the disease slowly eats away at the flesh. In time, the hands become only stumps and the face is deformed with ulcers. The victim eventually dies after a slow and painful process.

I remember so clearly how it all started. One morning after I woke up and was getting ready to go to work, I noticed on the back of my hand a small, white, scaly spot. At first I didn't think much of it. It itched a bit. Perhaps it was a bug bite or something. I ignored it, figuring that it would soon go away. But instead it only grew more and more noticeable. After a few days I wasn't able to hide its presence any more. My family saw the blemish, and although they refused to believe what they feared, they nevertheless encouraged and sent me to the priest to have my hand examined.

Unfortunately, I didn't have the benefit of the doctors you have today. When a medical condition had to be diagnosed, we went to see the priest. His job, amongst many others, was to examine the condition and prescribe any treatment necessary or, as it was in my case, to suggest a temporary quarantine to see if the blemish either goes away or gets worse.

For a week I was basically alone. My family fed and took care of me, but they were not allowed to come close to me. It was a terrible week—a week of waiting, watching and praying. I don't know how many times I looked at my hand to see if that spot had gone away, but if anything, it had only gotten bigger! By the time the week was over, my hand was no better.

I came before the priest, fearing the absolute worst. He once again examined my hand and then said those words that my family and I had, until then, refused to consider: "Leper! You are unclean! Get out of the city!"

At the sound of those words, I tore my clothes in grief. My ears had never heard such terrible news. Those were words of literal death. From that time on, I was considered dead to my family, to my friends, and to my village. But it was even worse than that. During my life, leprosy was believed to be a sign that God, too, had rejected me. Abandoned by my friends, by my family, and by my God, I was alone in the deepest sense of the word.

I wandered for a while as a beggar; it was the only possible way for me to make a living. For the most part, people averted their eyes from me. I know...I used to turn my eyes from lepers. But now, I couldn't even look at myself. I became quite proficient at hiding those areas of my body that were particularly diseased. I was embarrassed by my ugly and disfigured body. I turned my face down and kept my diseased hands hidden. Oh, how I used to long for someone just to recognize me as a person by looking into my eyes! From time to time, someone showed me some pity by giving some money or a bit of food. Eventually, I grouped up with the only people who would accept me...other lepers.

Here is the real irony of the situation: You see, I'm a Samaritan. Those other lepers were all Jews. I will be the first to admit that I had no respect for those self-righteous Jews who thought they had all the answers. They, in turn, despised us Samaritans for being half Jews and for not worshiping God properly. There has been fighting between our people, both theologically and politically, for years.

And yet, for this group of lepers, all those differences seemed to dissolve in the overwhelming recognition that we were all utterly alone. We were rejected by our people and by our God. They say that misery loves company. I am living proof of that proverb. We needed the human companionship that we could at least offer to one other...even if no one else in the world would offer us such friendship.

We wandered from place to place begging, always leading our presence with those words: "UNCLEAN, UNCLEAN. Lepers!" By law we were to keep 150 feet away from everyone. And that was when we were downwind from them. (Incidentally, not to frighten any of you, but all of you are in a little bit of trouble. Even those of you who are congratulating yourselves for sitting in the back are too close for comfort.)

One day we heard that Jesus was coming to this town. They said that he performed miracles—even HEALED people! Even in our isolation, we had heard some fantastic stories about him. Were they true or just exaggerated tales? Here was a man of God who was said to speak words of new life. My hopes soared! I hoped that, possibly, here was a chance to start a new life. And yet, part of me held back. I had been disappointed so many times before. Could I bear being disappointed again? But, then again, what had I to lose? I was already considered dead to the world I knew.

And then, there he was, surrounded by his followers. Our group got as close as we dared and together called out as loud as we could, "Jesus, Master, have mercy on us!" Our noise must have caught his attention because the group of people stopped and Jesus turned to us. With a voice that rang with confidence and comfort, he told us to go and show ourselves to the priests.

Why did he tell us to go the priests? It was the priest who spoke those words that condemned me to a living death, and it was to him I needed to return in order to show that I had been healed. I needed to hear his words that would declare me alive and clean—words that would allow me to once again be reunited with my family and friends.

Perhaps it was the tone of his voice or the compassion that seemed to pour out from him, or it might have been his reputation that preceded him. But for whatever reason, we did as he commanded, even though when we left his presence, we were still very much diseased. But something amazing happened as we headed to see the priests. I first noticed it in one my companions. His hand had been totally restored! For a few wonderful moments we all looked and held each other in disbelief. It was true! We had been healed! The others began to run toward the priest in order to show themselves to him. I was about to follow when something held me back. Sure, I wanted to go; I wanted to see my family again! I wanted to tell the whole world that I was alive! But I needed to do something else first.

I ran back to Jesus, and for the first time as far back as I could remember, I touched a man who was not a leper. And he allowed me to touch him. Yes, I am a Samaritan, and I was hugging the feet of a Jewish rabbi...and I didn't care in the least. Those differences became insignificant. Because of Jesus, I was brought to life once again! Even a priest could wait a little while so that I could give thanks to He who deserved the glory for this wonderful event.

But my presence seemed to trouble Jesus. He asked, "Were not ten made clean? But the other nine, where are they? Was none of them found to return and give praise to God except this foreigner?" Then he turned to me specifically, and I will never forget his words: "Get up and go on your way; your faith has made you well."[25]

Since then, I have often reflected on those words. How was I made well in a way that my other companions were not? Certainly, they all received healing too. I have come to this conclusion: yes, we were all cleansed from our leprosy, but it was Jesus who made me well in the most complete sense. Being cleansed of my leprosy allowed me to return to my family and friends, but I also returned to a relationship with God. When I returned to give thanks to Jesus, I recognized and expressed my gratitude to God for intervening in my life. I think that is what Jesus meant when he said, "Your faith has made you well."

Since being cured of physical leprosy, I have discovered another kind of leprosy in my life. It eats away at my very being and alienates me from God and

---

[25] Luke 17:17-19

others. I'm afraid the news will be bad. There is a strain of this disease that is extremely contagious and always fatal. In fact, we have all contracted the disease. Its symptoms are varied. Sometimes it shows itself by very subtle means; other times it is very obvious. But whether subtle or obvious, it is rooted in disobedience to God.

The good news is that unlike those of my age who said that leprosy was a sign that God had abandoned me, God has not left us alone with this fatal disease. Just as Jesus came to me and offered me healing, he can offer to you healing. You need only turn to him in faith.

But don't just stop there. Complete healing takes place when you recognize the working of God in your life and give God the credit for it. I know that it is so easy to take things for granted and not to give thanks. Many of us never truly realize what we have until it is taken away from us. I know because for a while, it was all taken away from me. But Jesus gave it all back to me. No longer do I yell out: "UNCLEAN! UNCLEAN!"

The words I now proclaim are: "BLESS THE LORD, O MY SOUL, AND FORGET NOT ALL HIS BENEFITS...

O BLESS THE LORD!" [26]

(Exit)

---

[26] Psalm 103:2

Discussion Questions: The Grateful Leper

In the first century, leprosy carried with it a terrible stigma. What conditions today might carry with it a similar shame?

Lepers experienced intense loneliness, rejection, isolation and abandonment in all aspects of their lives—not only from friends and family but, so they believed, even from God. Have you ever encountered a deep sense of loneliness?

Shared suffering can be the unlikely catalyst that draws dissimilar people together. Why is this true?

Remember that the other nine were also healed. But a special blessing was reserved for the one who returned. How is gratitude healing? What did the Samaritan receive that the other nine did not?

ZACCHAEUS

Since my Sunday School days, the story of Zacchaeus, that "wee little man," is one that I have treasured. When I began writing in this genre, I wondered how his story could become a monologue that expresses God's love for one who is rejected by others.

I used a simple table and stool set off to one side with coins, paper, and a letter (scroll) on the table. Center stage and toward the back, I used a short step ladder to represent the sycamore tree.

This monologue opens up with Randy Newman's 1977 song, "Short People." After a few moments of the song, it abruptly ends with a scratch, allowing Zacchaeus to begin his dialogue. Later, the sound of an approaching crowd plays to get Zacchaeus' attention. Also, the voice of Jesus from offstage invites Zacchaeus to come down. Later, that same voice announces that salvation has come to this house.

ZACCHAEUS - UP A TREE

(Zacchaeus enters with music of "Short People." After the first couple of lines, the music scratches and Zacchaeus begins his monologue.)

Boy, how I hate that song! The author must have been six-foot-three! Only those who are actually short could possibly know what it's like. I remember the names I was called and the teasing I suffered when I was a kid: "Hey, shorty!" "Hey, Zach, could you do up my sandals, seeing as you are in the area?" Then there were the stupid jokes: "Zacchaeus: the guy related to Knee-high-miah."

As a teenager, I managed to put up with it, assuming I was eventually going to grow. I thought, and hoped, that my growth spurt was just a little delayed. Unfortunately, it never came, and I remained the shortest guy in town.

Adults sometimes accuse young people of name calling and treating others who are different from them with cruelty. Let me tell you something: adults are no better…in fact they are worse because they know what they are doing and the hurt they cause, but they do it anyway!

Perhaps one of the most painful of insults was the way they would tease me about my name: "Hey Zacchaeus! Why did your folks give you that name? You are many things, but the 'righteous one' you most certainly are not! Who you fooling anyway?"

Well, by the time I was fifteen or sixteen, I had enough of it! I didn't need to take all that ribbing! I may be small, but I'm resilient and tough. And so I began to compensate for my size, putting my considerable energy and organizational skills to good work. They may be taller, but I can see farther.

I'm no genius, but I saw something that most of my neighbors missed. If you want to get anywhere in this world, then you need to make friends with those who are in power. The "real" tall people were the Romans. They had the control; they were the ones with the money; they were the ones with a real future. If I could align myself with them, then it wouldn't matter what others thought of my height.

When the opportunity came, I grabbed at it with both hands. It seemed like a godsend. The Romans needed a chief tax collector for the area of Jericho! What an opportunity! Jericho is a leading city, with a large population, and many traders from other countries would have to pay import taxes if they wanted to do business in this town. And as the chief tax collector, I would be responsible for all the other collectors in the area! If I could just land that job, I would be in "hog heaven," pardon the very un-kosher phrase.

Oh sure, I had to lay out a sizable amount of money to the Romans just to get the job. I sold most of my meager assets and made sizable promises, but those debts would quickly disappear once I started raking in a profit. *(He makes some quick calculations on sheet of paper.)* Well, let's see, first I would have to charge each citizen the required Roman taxes. Then of course, I would have to add a flat rate in order to cover the cost of getting this job. Then, quite naturally, I would need to add a percentage on top of that to cover my salary. Hmmmm...five percent, ten percent, let's call it fifteen percent! And, again naturally, as the chief tax collector,

I would also get some of the profits those collectors who worked under me raked in. No question about it: this was going to make me rich!

But you know what the best thing about this job was? I would now have the chance to get back at those who teased and needled me for years! Oh, that felt so *good*. Even better was that there was nothing they could do about it. Why? Because standing right next to me were two of the biggest, badest, meanest Roman legionaries you could imagine.

Yes, this job made for good money, but it did not make for good friends. Of course, my neighbors didn't take too kindly to my new role. But that didn't bother me too much. When, in the span of human history, has anyone liked a tax collector? But the job has to be done, and why shouldn't I be the one to profit from it? Of course, some had even darker opinions of my chosen occupation. The Romans were the occupying and unwelcome foreigners in this country. Working with them made me, in some people's eyes, a traitor and a collaborator.

Still, there were times that I would look up from my ledgers and see people walking down the streets, young boys playfully kicking a ball down the street, two men having a friendly conversation as they stepped into the inn across the way for a drink, or a married couple obviously in love and oblivious to the world around them. (*He wistfully imagines what it would be like while unconsciously playing with coins on table. He is then suddenly aware of the coins...*) But who needs all that? I've got my business to run, and I will certainly have the last laugh!

(He notices mail on desk.) What's this? It looks like a letter from Levi. I haven't heard from him for years. Levi is a colleague of mine who collects taxes north of here, in the Galilee area. I met him some time ago at a tax collectors' convention in Jerusalem. Oh, you think that's odd? I bet you have friends in your occupation that you look forward to meeting at vocational gatherings. Where else am I going to learn about the latest Roman tax and the newest changes and forms in the tax laws? Besides, we tax collectors don't make too many friends in the communities we gather taxes from, so we have to look elsewhere for our friendships. I wonder why Levi is writing me now.

(He opens and reads the letter, mumbling until he gets to the significant part.) How you doing...hope family is fine...things going well here...Oh, this is interesting. Levi has got himself connected with a new rabbi in the Galilee area. His name is Jesus. *(He looks up.)* I've heard about this guy! Rumor has it he has done some pretty exciting things. They also say he doesn't pre-judge people. *(Cynically, he says,)* Yeah right. From what I've heard, he has also said some stuff that has made the authorities, both religious and civil, a little upset. *(He returns to letter.)* Hey! Levi says he is coming to Jerusalem and will be passing through Jericho on his way. Furthermore, Levi writes that he would be glad to introduce me to this rabbi.

I wonder when he will be arriving. *(He searches the letter for an answer as the background sounds of a crowd begins to grow louder.)* What's that sound? Jesus? Here already? Well, I have just got to check this out for myself! *(He quickly clears the table of coins and moves in the direction of noise. At stage right, he starts*

67

jumping up and down, as if trying to see over the shoulders of crowd. At the same time, he keeps backing up because the crowd is moving). What's going on? Is it Jesus? I can't see! Let me through, please! *(After being continually rebuffed, he looks around, spots the tree stage left and runs to base of it.)* Perhaps if I can just get high enough in this tree, I will be able to get a glimpse of him as he walks by.

I'm sure I used to do this all the time back when I was a kid, but I can't remember. And climbing one of these things in a robe can't be the easiest and most dignified of exercises. Still, I gave up caring about what people thought of me a long, long time ago. *(He struggles to get up the tree; once there, he realizes that he has become a somewhat easy target for ridicule.)* Oh, no! In my rashness to see this Jesus, I've left my booth without my usual Roman escort. *(Addressing those at the base of the tree, he says,)* Don't mind me; I'm just trying to get a good view. Hey! Be nice or I'll charge extra the next time you have to come to see me! Ouch! *(He grab his forehead.)* That rock hurt! *(He tries to hide behind a tree branch; after a moment, he takes a peek.)* Hello? Who is this now looking up?

(A voice offstage says, "Zacchaeus, hurry on down, for I am having lunch with you today.")

Hurry on down? I was so excited, so stunned, I nearly fell out of the tree! I can't remember the last time anyone wanted to have lunch with me. People stayed in my presence only for the required seconds it took for them to pay their taxes. Then they left quickly, feeling soiled by my presence. But he wants to eat with me!

I'm sure my eagerness to have him over at my house made me look even sillier than I looked in the tree. In my enthusiasm, I would run ahead a little distance, and then run back to him, and then run ahead a little further. I wanted him to get to my house soon; I feared that he would change his mind.

I won't bore you with the details of our meal or of the conversation that occurred. To tell you the truth, they were almost incidental. Oh, it's not that his words weren't important, but it's what he did that meant the most! He made me feel like I truly mattered...something I haven't felt in a very, very long time!

For so many years, I had treated others like they had treated me. If I didn't matter to them, then they didn't matter to me either! But Jesus showed me another side of myself that I thought was long gone. If I was valuable to God, then, by the same token, I could no longer treat others with carelessness and thoughtlessness. I found myself saying it even before I realized it, but I meant every word of it:

"Lord, half of my possessions I will give back to the poor and if I have defrauded anyone of anything, I will pay back four times as much!"[27] There, I said it. I must have broken a new record for doing and saying the most silly things in one day. Everyone must think I have gone totally crazy! But I only care what he thinks!

(The voice offstage says, "Today salvation has come to this house because he too is a son of Abraham.")[28]

---

[27] Luke 19:8
[28] Luke 19:9

ZACCHAEUS: *Luke 19:1-10*

(He falls to his knees.) I am a son of Abraham?! I am one of God's chosen?! I, who has been overlooked and rejected by so many: have I not been forgotten by God? *(He stands.)* I may be small, but I am not too small for God to see me. You know something else? With God's help, I think I can truly live up to my name.

Zacchaeus: the righteous one. I kind of like that.

(Exit)

Discussion Questions: Zacchaeus

Desperation can lead people to do some surprising and interesting things. While I have speculated on what led Zacchaeus to become a tax collector, his attempt to see Jesus was clearly an act of desperation. Can you think of other biblical characters that took extraordinary measures to connect with God?

Many people suffer from a sense of worthlessness. Zacchaeus, a short man, had become used to feeling that way, but when Jesus took notice of him, it radically changed his life. Taking notice of someone can have transformative power. Why? And when we are convinced that God has taken notice of us, even greater transformation is possible. Why is that true?

What did Jesus say or do that prompted Zacchaeus to express radical generosity?

PETRINE MONOLOGUES

I developed this collection of three monologues over the course of several years. The first began as a meditation for a Maundy Thursday service that incorporated the Lord's Supper into the monologue itself. A couple of years later, I realized, albeit rather slowly, that this was by no means the end of Peter's story. And so, on Easter morning, I shared the second of these monologues that picks up after Peter's denial and follows him through the trial, crucifixion, and resurrection of Jesus. You might think I would have learned my lesson, but it took another couple of years before I realized again that Peter's story was not yet complete. On a Pentecost Sunday, I told the remaining part of Peter's story that continues at the end of the gospels and moves into the book of Acts.

One of the inevitable challenges in trying to develop some kind of a chronology of events during Passion week is that the gospels are not always clear about what happened and when. I was not intending to develop a harmony between the gospels in this monologue but to share with the congregation a series of events from Peter's life that took place during Passion Week.

In the first monologue, the first several days of Passion Week are told in retrospect; Peter is remembering the different events from Sunday through Wednesday. When Thursday arrives, we move into present tense and action is described as it is taking place. When Jesus offers the bread and the cup, Peter, in front of the congregation, really does break the bread and offer the cup. After the words are spoken, "In remembrance of me," the congregation is invited to participate in the Last Supper. (In my congregation setting, we received the sacrament by intinction, in which we invited the congregation to come to the same table where Peter and, by inference, the other disciples and Jesus were sitting). After all have been served, and after an appropriate moment of silence, Peter then continues the monologue.

In the second monologue, Peter enters dancing and singing until he realizes there are people present. As before, Peter tells the Easter Story in retrospect. As he retells the story, he shows the chaos, pain, fear, confusion, and then great joy in both voice and action. When telling the story of the crucifixion, he uses his staff as the horizontal beam of the cross, resting it on his shoulders with his arms spread wide. When Jesus finally appears, Peter speaks the words spoken to him using a different voice to accentuate his words. Similarly, when Thomas speaks, Peter uses more of an intellectual's cynical voice. As in the first monologue, communion is incorporated into the dialogue. This time the meal being described with Jesus is when Jesus offers breakfast to the disciples on the shores of Galilee.

I like to think that Peter enjoyed singing. So at the beginning of the second monologue and at the end of the third, I sing. You could certainly choose other songs that fit your context and are familiar to you and your congregation. The ones I used in the script worked for me.

The third monologue is probably the longest I have written. It contains seven stories about Peter from the book of Acts. I suggest that as you tell each story, move to a different part of the stage to help delineate them.

Peter is such a remarkable individual. He is developed as a character in Scripture with all his strengths and weaknesses. We are shown his powerful declarations of faith and his all-too-human flaws. Perhaps that is why we identify with him so much. These monologues seek to reveal that wonderful disciple, whom Jesus loved, patiently taught, forgave, and entrusted to "feed his sheep."

PETER

PETRINE MONOLOGUE PART I

Some of you probably know me, but I'm afraid I
don't know many of you. Peter is my name. I used to be
a fisherman, but that was a few years ago, before he
came. Things have never quite been the same since
then. These three years have been some of the most
exciting in my life. But this last week has easily
outdone everything that happened before, and it's only
Thursday! So much has happened that I can't even
begin to guess what the rest of the week will be like!
It's Passover in Jerusalem, and everyone seems to be
here to participate in the festival!

It all began on Sunday. What a day that was! Oh,
I've attended a few Passovers in Jerusalem, but I've
seen nothing like this! Talk about enthusiasm! Jesus
came into Jerusalem riding on a simple donkey. People
from all over were waving their hands, praising God,
and singing, "Hosanna to the Son of David! Blessed is
he who comes in the name of the Lord! Hosanna in the
highest!" Many were placing palm branches on the
ground before him to signify Jesus' kingship. We
disciples were sure that Jesus was going to finally
proclaim himself King of Israel and take the country
back from those Gentile Romans and the self-righteous
Pharisees. People were finally beginning to recognize
Jesus as the promised one of the God...the Messiah!

On Sunday evening, we returned to Bethany, which
is a couple of miles right outside of Jerusalem. I suspect
we stayed there because Jesus had some good friends
living in Bethany, and during this time of year, it is so
crowded in Jerusalem that it is very hard to find a place
to stay in the city. I was so excited that evening; I didn't

get much sleep. On Monday morning, we got up and began once again to go toward Jerusalem. On the way into the city, Jesus saw a fig tree and wanted something to eat. When he saw that the tree had no fruit on it, he cursed the tree! We all thought that was a little strange, but after following Jesus for three years, we had come to expect the strange.

When we got to Jerusalem we went to the Temple to pray as we often did. But this time something quite different happened. Jesus became infuriated! He saw the money changers and the animal sellers inside the temple area and he got really angry. He made a whip and drove them out of the temple saying, "This place is a house of prayer, but you have made it into a den of thieves!"[29] I'm sure that made the religious leaders upset! Jesus was beginning to turn all of Jerusalem upside down!

On our way into Jerusalem the following day, Tuesday, we noticed the fig tree Jesus had cursed the previous day had died! Jesus told us that with faith, we could do virtually anything. After what I saw those previous two days I don't think I could have ever doubted Jesus.

We returned again to the Temple, and Jesus spent much of the day teaching us and anyone else who would listen. Most of what he said was in parables and stories. I didn't understand a lot of what he meant, but I did pick up on this: many of his stories were directed right at the Pharisees and scribes. He called them all sorts of names! Jesus must be very sure of himself and

---

[29] Matthew 21:13

his power, and he better be right, or we are all in a lot of trouble when they catch up with us.

Toward the end of the day, we were walking around the Temple, admiring its impressiveness. I pointed out some of the great stones and decorations to Jesus. But Jesus told us that in a very short time, all of the temple will be destroyed and the end of the world will come. It was all very confusing and I didn't understand. But he told us we needed to be careful and not believe everything we hear or follow everyone we see. Instead, we were supposed to wait faithfully for God's timing.

Jesus thought that it might be nice to have a quieter day, so we spent most of yesterday in Bethany. But even while we were there, a very unusual thing happened. I haven't quite figured it out yet. (As you may gather, this happens to me a fair amount.) We were staying at the home of Mary, Martha, and Lazarus, whom Jesus had previously raised from the dead. While we were there, Mary took a very expensive bottle of perfume—one that would have cost me a year's worth of fishing—and poured it over Jesus' feet! All of us were pretty upset about her wastefulness. If she wanted to do something charitable, she should have sold the perfume and given the money to the poor. We thought that was pretty good advice. After all, Jesus had once told a rich young man to do just that. Jesus, however, had another idea. He told us not to bother her because she was preparing his body for burial. Another one of his riddles! Sometimes I feel so stupid when I don't understand what he is saying.

Well, that brings us to today. We returned to Jerusalem this morning for the Passover meal. Jesus sent John and me to go and prepare the meal at a home that he had already chosen. That's where we are now.

(He takes a seat at the communion table.) I'm sitting here waiting for the Passover meal to begin, but Jesus has just gotten up and...no...I don't believe it! He has begun to wash our feet. That's ridiculous! He shouldn't be doing that! *(He looks at his feet where Jesus is kneeling.)* "Lord, you are never going to wash my feet!" *(He pauses.)* "If washing means that I am part of you, then I want to be given a complete bath, not just a foot wash!" *(He pauses again.)* "So I only need my feet cleaned to be a part of you. And we are all supposed to be servants in the manner like you just showed to us."

Well, here comes the Passover meal. Jesus took the bread, prayed over it, and...uh oh. He is doing something different, something special again. *"This is my body which is broken for you. All of you eat of it in remembrance of me. This is my blood which is shed for you and for the forgiveness of sins. All of you drink of it in remembrance of me."*[30]

(The congregation partakes in communion with Peter.)

I wonder what that all meant. Jesus looks very tired and even upset this evening. What's that? One of us is going to betray him?! NEVER! I was so confused that I asked John, who was sitting next to Jesus, to ask him who he was talking about. Jesus said something about the person he hands a piece of bread to—Judas Iscariot. Judas left, but I was so upset, tired, and confused that I hardly noticed.

---

[30] Luke 22: 17-18, 20

After Judas left, Jesus began to talk again. He said that he would be leaving us soon and going to a place where none of us can follow. "Lord, why can't I go with you now? I would gladly die for you!" *(He pauses.)* "Deny you?! I could never deny you once, Lord, much less three times!"

Despite my confusion and exhaustion, Jesus continues to speak, but this all sounds much better. He is telling us that he will ask God to send the Holy Spirit to comfort us and to let us know we are never alone.

The Passover meal is finally over, and we closed the meal with a hymn. Jesus wants to go over to the Garden of Gethsemane right outside the city's walls to pray for a while. He always did like that spot. Perhaps being there and praying for a while will make him feel better. John, James, and I have been invited to pray with him. Jesus, you look so upset. I wish I could comfort you in some way, but I am so tired. So much has happened this past week. *(He falls asleep)*

What's going on?! There are Romans, and Pharisees, and...and...*Judas* is leading them. Judas is greeting Jesus, no it's not a greeting...it's the betrayal that Jesus spoke of! No! I won't let it happen! I may be just a fisherman, but I'm going to put up a fight!

What...you don't want me to fight, Lord? But they are taking you away from us! I can't fight, but I...I can't stay either. I'm running away. But not too far away. I'm following at a distance to find out what is going to happen.

They take him to the home of Caiaphas, the high priest. It sure is cold this evening. There is a fire in the courtyard over there...maybe I can warm myself there and still look inconspicuous. Besides, I need some time to think and try to sort out my next move. So much has happened these past few days. *(He speaks to another person at the fire.)* "Huh? No, I don't know the man over there. Never met him before in my life." *(He returns to his reflection.)* Whatever happened to last Sunday? I thought for sure that we were going to take over Jerusalem with Jesus as our new leader. Where did all those cheering voices go? *(To another, he says,)* "What? Like I told that other person, I know nothing about that man over there." *(Again speaking to himself, he says,)* Have these past three years really been worth it? Jesus has sure taught me a whole lot. Yet, I'm not sure anyone could have guessed that it would be ending like this. *(Speaking with anger, he says,)* "Not again! I don't care if I do have his accent! I have never met that man and I want nothing to do with him! Go away and leave me alone!"

Oh God, the cock is crowing just as Jesus promised it would after I denied him. I did it. I actually did it. I've denied the one person who has loved me in a way no one else could. Jesus, Jesus...I am so sorry. God, what have I done?! What have I done?!

(He runs off stage.)

PETER

Discussion Questions: Petrine Part I

(As suggested in the introduction to the Petrine monologues, this discussion might be appropriate during Holy Week.)

It must have been quite a roller-coaster ride for the disciples—starting on Sunday and riding through to Jesus' arrest in the Garden of Gethsemane with all the ups and downs in between. Using a piece of paper, chart the ups and downs of Passion week. How is your journey of faith similar to your completed chart?

In this story, and elsewhere in the gospel narrative, Peter is constantly confused and puzzled by the actions and words of Jesus. Does this comfort or frustrate you? Why?

When Peter finally recognizes his own betrayal of Jesus he is devastated. In what ways do we deny Jesus—not just once but frequently?

PETRINE MONOLOGUE PART II

An Easter Story

(Peter enters singing and dancing.) "Hallelujah! I will sing unto the Lord, for he has triumphed gloriously, the horse and the rider he has thrown into the sea. The Lord reigneth! Blessed be the rock and may the God of my salvation be exalted!"

Oh, hello. Good to see some of you again! I saw some of you just a few days ago. For the rest of you, my name is Simon, although many call me Peter...yeah him. I'm sure some of you have heard of me before. I'm the guy who is constantly putting his foot in his mouth. But not today. Oh, it's a good day. No, it isn't: it's a GREAT day!

How's that? You haven't heard? Hasn't anyone told you what has happened? And I thought word traveled fast in these parts. Well, he did it! He actually did it! What was that? Who did what? Now, that's a good question. Maybe before I tell you, I should first back up a little.

I shared with many of you what took place last week. It was quite a week—full of excitement. It had its ups and downs. But on Thursday, the high priest had Jesus arrested and brought to trial...if you could call what they did to him a trial. I was out in the courtyard of Caiaphas' house when I denied him three times. I was so ashamed that I ran out on you last week. I couldn't face anyone, including myself, for hours.

Inside, they mocked and ridiculed him. Finally, wanting to kill him, they took him over to the Roman governor's house, Pontius Pilate. As bad as they wanted

83

to, they couldn't kill Jesus without Roman approval. But Pilate could find nothing about him deserving of the death penalty. But during his interrogation, he discovered that Jesus had come from the Galilee area, and since King Herod was in Jerusalem, and this was part of his jurisdiction, Pilate transferred Jesus to Herod's palace. After taunting Jesus for a while, Herod sent him packing back to Pilate, wanting nothing to do with him. Nobody wants to deal with Jesus face-to-face. I think a lot of people treat Jesus that way.

Once again, Pilate interviewed Jesus. Pilate's wife had warned him not to have anything to do with this man, but these noisy Jewish leaders were inciting the crowd to have him killed. But Pilate came up with a plan that he thought would get him out of this dilemma. Every year, he allows one criminal to go free, and so he offered the people a choice between Jesus and a criminal named Barabbas. He certainly thought they would choose Jesus. But, much to his surprise, they chose Barabbas.

Exasperated, he washed his hands of the whole affair, as if it could be that easy, and sentenced Jesus to death. But those given such a sentence are also beaten, tortured, and humiliated. A cruel crown of thorns was placed upon his head; he was stripped and scourged. And then, as the final token of punishment, he had to carry the tool of his own execution to the top of Golgotha, a hill. There, they nailed him to that cross and dropped it into the ground.

(He places his staff on shoulders with his arms spread out.) Crucifixion is not a pretty sight. The poor souls who are crucified die not from exposure or from blood loss but from exhaustion and suffocation. In

order to breathe, they must pull their weight up with their pierced and pinned arms and legs. During those painful hours, Jesus said little, but when he did speak, he spoke in volumes. "*Eloi, Eloi, lama sabachtenai*; My God, my God, why have you forsaken me? Today you will be with me in paradise. Father, forgive them, for they know not what they do. It is finished. Into your hands I commit my spirit."[31]

(He removes his staff from his shoulder.) And with those words, he died and the earth and sun died with him. There was an earthquake; the sun went black, as did my heart. A day and a night, another day and another night passed. We hid in fear; we hid in despair; we hid because we were as lost as anyone could be. Our only comfort existed in one another's tears.

There was one, Joseph of Arimathea, a wealthy and pious man who asked Pilate if he could bury him. But it was late on the day before Sabbath and there was not time to properly prepare his body. A quick wrapping, a few prayers, and the cold, hard stone of death were all we could give our teacher. As the stone rolled over the entrance, it buried all our hopes with it.

And so we waited. For what? Who knows...for our hearts to begin to beat again? For the madness of grief imbedded in our minds to give way to something...something...we didn't know what. It was a Sabbath to forget and, yet, one we would never be able to forget.

On Sunday, there were things to be done. Life continues even when we don't know how. A few of the women left early in the morning to finish what could

---

[31] Mark 15:34, Luke 23:43, Luke 23:34, Luke 23:46, John 19:30

not be completed before the Sabbath. They took the necessary spices in order to properly bury him—he whom we had once called Lord. But before too long, they came running back inside with incredible news! They found no guards at the tomb where Jesus was laid. They found no stone covering the tomb. And most shocking of all, they had found no body! But they did find angels who said that Jesus was no longer in the grave; he was alive! Naturally, we thought the women were nuts!

But they did see something, so John and I ran as quickly as we could to the grave. John is a little younger than I and beat me to the tomb by a few seconds. When I got there, he was standing at the door of the tomb looking in, but he was apparently too scared to enter. With all the tact I am famous for, I pushed him aside and stumbled in.

It was true! There was no body! The burial cloths were there, but Jesus' body was gone! If someone had taken him, they certainly wouldn't have left the wrappings behind! We left stunned, confused and bewildered. What did this all mean? Returning to the others, we told them what we saw.

As we talked this over, two other disciples (Cleopas and a friend of his) showed up with news that was just as startling and just as unnerving: They were walking from Jerusalem to Emmaus, about a seven-mile journey west of the city. Like the rest of us, they were pretty shocked and upset by the past couple of days. While they were talking with each other about the events that had transpired, a third man joined them and asked what they were talking about. Surprised that this stranger didn't seem to know anything about the recent events,

Cleopas told him how Jesus, whom they thought and hoped was the Christ, had just been killed. The stranger, it turned out, was a teacher and began to share with the two men all about the Messiah and the prophesies found in Scriptures concerning him. When they arrived in Emmaus, the disciples invited the stranger to spend the night. At supper, when their guest gave thanks and broke the bread, they finally recognized him. It was JESUS. And as soon as he was recognized, he disappeared, but then, so did the disciples. Even though it was evening they ran back to Jerusalem to share the news with us!

Jesus alive? Could it possibly be true? Did we dare believe it? All of us were talking at once—trying to remember what Jesus had said and trying to recall those Scriptures that might bring some light and hope into our darkness and despair. In the midst of all this noise and commotion, Jesus himself showed up! Talk about a conversation stopper! We were frightened, and yet...

(In different voice, Peter recites,) "Shalom. Peace to you. Why are you troubled and frightened? See my hands and my feet, it is I. Handle me and see that I am flesh and bones."[32] And we touched him, tentative at first, but our joy soon replaced our fear and timid touches turned into bear hugs. Jesus even joined us for a meal of broiled fish!

Unfortunately, Thomas wasn't there. He missed out on seeing Jesus that first time. Later, after Jesus had left, Thomas shows up. He entered the room, still wearing that sad expression that we had all worn so much during the past couple of days. He looked up to

---

[32] Luke 24:36-37 (paraphrase)

see our smiles and laughter and immediately concluded that we had all finally gone over the edge of sanity. We tried to explain what had happened, but Thomas was ever the intellectual empiricist: *(In different voice, Peter says,) "Unless I see in his hands the print of the nails, and place my finger in the mark of the nails, and place my hand in his side, I will not believe."*[33] Oh boy, I was going to look forward to watching that moment!

Sure enough, about eight days later, we were in that same room, this time with Thomas. And like before, Jesus showed up. He went right up to Thomas, *(In different voice, Peter says,) "Put your finger here, Thomas, and see my hands; put out your hand, and place it in my side, do not be faithless, but believe."* Well, Thomas may be slow to believe, but when he does, he goes all the way. *(In different voice, he says,) "My Lord, and my God!"*

Later, the eleven of us left Jerusalem and returned to our home area of Galilee. The excitement and glow of the news had not worn off, but there was nothing left for us to do in Jerusalem. Having spent so much time together over the last few years, we could hardly be separated from one another now. We spent hours talking and sharing, remembering stories and Scriptures we learned from Jesus. But as you might have guessed, I tend to be a little on the energetic side. I can't stay cooped up too long or I'll go nuts! Finally, one night I turned to the other ten and announced, "I'm going fishing!" Well, I'm not sure I meant that to be an invitation for all the others, but you know how it is with men and fishing.

---

[33] John 20:25-28

So we went. I don't know why we went when we did; it was a lousy night for fishing. Time and time again we put out our nets only to pull them back in as empty as they were when we cast them. Fishing had never been this bad...except on one other occasion. By daybreak, my friends were beginning to grumble that this was a bad idea. We were just pulling in our nets for the last time and preparing to head home for some shut-eye, when a voice from the shore called out to us, *(In different voice, he says,) "Did you catch anything?"*

That question is common enough among fishermen. And, hey, I like to tell a good fish story as much as the next angler. But this fellow probably wanted to buy some of our catch so he could have breakfast. Unfortunately, we didn't have any. "No. Maybe you better try a different boat!" Well, the stranger suggested instead that we throw our nets on the other side of the boat. We all thought that a little silly. This guy was about 100 yards away; how could he see where the fish were? Still, what did we have to lose?

Before we knew it, the whole boat was leaning to the right side under the strain of fish that filled our net. It was then that John finally understood what was happening. He nudged me. "It's the Lord!" he said. That's it! I was no longer interested in the fish, my exhaustion, or my hunger. It was Jesus. I didn't even care if I got wet. I jumped in the water and swam the hundred yards to shore. John was right. It is Jesus and he had prepared breakfast for us.

That breakfast brought back the joyous memories of earlier meals we shared around a fire.

(The congregation partakes in communion with Peter.)

89

Oh, the things Jesus had taught us! That morning, we sang and ate, laughed and dreamed. Later, after breakfast, Jesus pulled me aside and asked me, *(In different voice, Peter says,)* *"Simon, son of John, do you love me?"*[34] That question hurt, not because he doubted my love but because it reminded me of my own fickleness and how I had denied him back in Jerusalem. I shuffled my feet for a moment and then I said, "Lord, you know that I love you." And he said to me, *"Feed my sheep."* Then he said it a second time, *"Simon, son of John, do you love me?"* With more confidence this time, I answered, "Yes, Lord, you know I love you." And he said, *"Tend my sheep."* Once more he said, *"Simon, son of John, do you love me?"* I had denied him three times, was he giving me the opportunity to confess my love for him three times? Finally, I responded, "Lord, you know everything; you know that I love you." And again he said, *"Feed my sheep."*

Over the years, that call has continued to echo in my memory. Despite my failure and denial, Jesus forgave and re-commissioned me to feed his sheep. They certainly aren't mine. *Humph*! I'm probably one of the most stubborn sheep in the flock! And yet, Jesus gave me something to do.

The last day with Jesus will always be one to remember. He led us up into the mountains. The mountains always held a special place for Jesus and for us. So much had happened over the last three years on the mountains. Jesus often took us there to pray. He

[34] John 21:15ff

sometimes preached on their hillsides. He met Elijah and Moses upon a mountain. But of all the mountain excursions, this one will be the hardest to forget. When we got to the top, he turned to us and said, *(In different voice, Peter says,)* "*All authority in heaven and on earth has been given to me. Go therefore and make disciples of all nations, baptizing them in the name of the Father and of the Son and of the Holy Spirit, and teaching them to obey everything that I have commanded you. And remember, I am with you always, to the end of the age.*"[35]

And then, he simply ascended into heaven. He left. But not really. I have never forgotten that promise. *I am with you always.* Indeed, that is what this day is about. Not even death can keep him from being with us! He is Risen!

---

[35] Matthew 28:18-20

PETER

(Exit)

Discussion Questions: Petrine Part II

Both Herod and Pilate tried to avoid dealing with Jesus. What is it about Jesus that makes us try to keep him at arm's length?

Because we believe that Jesus was resurrected, we often don't take time to reflect on the suffering that Jesus endured on the cross on our behalf. Find several examples of crucifixion scenes and meditate on them. What emotions come to the surface?

The reaction to the news of Jesus' resurrection is varied among the disciples. Shock, surprise, incredulity, and doubt name a few. What others can you imagine?

Jesus' three questions to Peter are a form of commissioning. *Feed my sheep.* On the mountain, Jesus commissions all the disciples to go to all the nations and make disciples. Is some form of commissioning inherent in being a disciple of Jesus? If so, what does your commission look like?

PETRINE MONOLOUGE PART III

With Peter on Pentecost

Shalom my friends! Peace. It is good to see you once again! This is now my third time to worship and to visit with you. One of my greatest joys is to visit other churches to see what God is doing among them. And God is among you my friends, never doubt that!

Earlier I shared with you a part of my story. *Humph*! My story has more ups and downs than the mountains in Israel! But by the grace and mercy of God, I stand here ready and able to confess that Jesus Christ remains my Lord and Savior. I have already told you about that final week in Jerusalem before he was crucified. Then, almost two months ago I shared with you how he rose from the dead and how he met with us on several occasions. But the story is not yet over. If I had left it there I would have been excluding some of the best parts! So I have returned to continue where I left off.

Jesus told us before he ascended into heaven to wait for the coming of the Holy Spirit. And so we waited. There were the eleven disciples (Judas, of course was no longer with us), and many other men and women. We waited, not knowing quite what to expect, but it didn't matter.

We spent much of our time together in prayer and study. Although we had spent three years with him, it wasn't until after his resurrection that so much of what he said made sense. We had to re-read our Scriptures, recall all that he said, and re-learn what it all meant in light of his coming alive!

It was at the feast of Pentecost that it happened.
Pentecost comes fifty days after Passover (thus its
name, "Penta"). It was the annual harvest festival and a
celebration of the anniversary of the day Moses
received the law on Mount Sinai. All of us were in an
upper room, talking, praying, and sharing. The room
began to shake, the wind began to blow, and...and...how
do I explain it? Tongues of fire rested on top of our
heads! I kid you not! You find that hard to believe?
Well, so did we!

And then we all started to speak in different
languages! John was speaking Egyptian, Matthew was
talking in Cyprian, Bartholomew was conversing
fluently in Mesopotamian, and I still don't know what
language Thomas was speaking! Now most of us knew
three languages, at least in some way. Aramaic is our
general conversing tongue. Hebrew is the language of
our Scriptures. And we spoke Greek often in our
conversations with the Romans and other outsiders. But
this was all new! Although I didn't understand what
everyone was saying, I knew they were praising God.
Because it was Pentecost, there were many people from
all over the empire in Jerusalem. Jerusalem is really
very cosmopolitan. And these people heard their native
languages being spoken!

There were some in Jerusalem who thought we
might be a little drunk with wine. But it was only nine
o'clock in the morning! Then I remembered what the
prophet Joel had written: In the last days, God will pour
out his Spirit on all flesh. We were living that
prophesy!

Pentecost! The celebration of this very old festival
now has new meaning for Christ's church! Just as it

celebrates the anniversary of the giving of the law to Moses so does this new Pentecost celebrate the receiving of the Spirit—the new law—into the hearts of everyone who calls upon the name of the Lord.

Well, no one has ever accused me of being shy. Taking my stand before the crowd, I preached my very first sermon. I suppose by Presbyterian *(Insert your denomination...)* standards it was adequate, if not perfect. For starters, it lacked a three-point outline, but God nevertheless used it to challenge the many people who were in Jerusalem. By the time that day was over, over 3,000 people were added to our "little" group.

Now you might have thought that with all this new spiritual insight, we might have given up on regular attendance at the temple. On the contrary! We saw the temple as an important part of our on-going worship, and I continued to go often for prayer and worship.

On one trip, John and I were climbing the steps to enter the temple area when we saw a cripple who was begging at the stairs. The entrance to the temple is a pretty good place to beg. People usually come and go from there in a generous spirit. Unfortunately, John and I didn't have any money with us that day. And that is what we told this poor fellow.

But what we did have was much better. I gave a knowing wink at John, and he nodded back. Then I looked the man square in the eye and said, "In the name of Jesus Christ of Nazareth, stand up and walk!"[36] Then, before he could refuse, I reached down, grabbed him by the hand, and pulled him to his feet! Right then and there, he began to run and jump and praise God.

---

[36] Acts 3:6

Well, as you can imagine, that caused quite a stir. People had seen this man as a crippled beggar for years. But now he was running around like a little kid! All this commotion began to draw a crowd. Not wishing to let such an opportune moment go by, I preached the second sermon of my career. And once again, more people came to believe in Jesus as the Messiah.

But while I was still speaking with the people, some of the temple authorities, who were often jealous keepers of their positions as the "all-knowing" teachers of scripture, came and arrested John and myself. We spent that night in jail! The next day we stood before the Sanhedrin, the highest ruling body in Israel, to answer for our so-called "crimes." After telling our story, and once again preaching Jesus even to these religious leaders (that took guts!), they only threatened us and let us go, warning us not to talk any more about Jesus. Well, given the choice between following the law of the Sanhedrin or the law of God—duh, tough choice—we kept telling others about Jesus.

By the grace of God, others continued to join our group and we began to share much of what we had: our food, our homes, our money. In a sense, it wasn't ours in the first place, it was all God's. So why wouldn't we share it with others?

But before you start to think everything was perfect, maybe I better share another story. One couple in our group, Ananias and his wife Sapphira, tried to cheat God. Like many of the people in our group, they sold some of their property and gave the proceeds to the growing church. But while they claimed to have given the church all of the proceeds, they had actually kept some of it for themselves. Their sin was not that they kept some of the money but that they lied about it to God. And for that sin, God struck them dead. That shook us all up. A profound sense of awe and of responsibility entered into the early church as a result of that. What was happening among us was not to be taken lightly.

Not too long after that, several of us were once again arrested by the Sanhedrin. I was becoming a regular criminal! Like before, they intended to interrogate us the following morning, but an angel released us during the night. The next morning, when the religious leaders ordered us to be brought before them, we couldn't be found! While they were wondering how we had escaped, word came that we were back out in the temple teaching, which is the very place we were when they had arrested us the previous day! We had returned, if you will, to the scene of our crime! They must have thought we were nuts!

They sent guards to get us, but they were afraid of the crowds who were beginning to hear and respond to the gospel we preached. No wanting to incur violence, we chose to go with them peacefully. Once again, the Sanhedrin warned us not to preach in the name of Christ. One of them, Gamaliel, spoke a little bit on our behalf, warning his colleagues that if this new movement was from God they could do nothing to stop it. In fact, they could find themselves even opposing God, which was not a particularly healthy prospect. Instead of killing us, which is what some of them wanted to do, they had us whipped and sent us out with a final warning.

The last thing they heard as we walked out their door was the sound of our rejoicing and giving praise to

God that we were considered worthy to suffer for the sake of Christ. I'm sure they definitely thought we were crazy!

Well, the church continued to grow and expand. Because of its growing size, we apostles designated a group of committed followers to help the needy. We called them deacons, and we began to spread out beyond Jerusalem. The first missionaries were sent out. Philip began preaching in Samaria and some miraculous things were taking place there. On behalf of the Jerusalem church, I went up north to see what he was doing there. Later, I traveled west to Lydda and Joppa, where God used me to heal one man who had been sick for eight years and a woman who had even died!

But those mission trips were still to other Jews. Looking back, I think God was preparing me for an even greater challenge. I was still in the coastal city of Joppa when it first began. I had been staying at a friend's house, and it was getting close to noon. Since it wasn't quite lunchtime yet, I went up on top of his roof. They have these great houses in Joppa; you can sit up on the roof and get a sun tan without the hassle of going down to the beach.

I was up there praying and waiting for lunch. I was beginning to get quite hungry! But in the middle of my praying, I had a vision. Call it a dream, a voice from God, call it whatever you want, but I am convinced that God was trying to tell me something. It's kind of hard to explain, but I will try.

In my vision, a great blanket was being lowered from heaven. It was as if a heavenly picnic table was being prepared for me. But the table before me was like nothing I had ever seen before! You know, of course, that Jews are prohibited from eating all sorts of foods. And it seemed to me that this blanket included just about every kind of forbidden food. And a voice from heaven said, "Get up and eat, Peter." Eeeeuuugh! My stomach turned at the very thought! I no longer was hungry. In fact, I was repulsed! "By no means Lord," I said, "for I have never eaten anything that is unclean or profane." But God said, "What I have made clean, you must not call profane."[37] This happened three different times! At the end of the last time, the blanket was taken back into heaven.

As you can imagine, I was curious as to what this all meant. Even as I was trying to sort through it all, a knock came on the door downstairs. God told me that there were three men at the door who wanted me to go with them, and I was to do so. It turns out they were the servants of a pious, but Roman centurion who wanted to hear the gospel story.

Well, this was certainly going to be a new experience! We Jews rarely had any dealings with Gentiles, but now I was being invited to go to one of their homes! Then I began to realize what that crazy dream was all about. The Gentiles, whom we had for years called impure and profane, were in the eyes of God just as worthy and in need of hearing the gospel as the Jews were! It was going to take a mindset adjustment, but I was determined to obey God.

I left with those three men and we traveled up the coast to Caesarea. When we arrived at his home, Cornelius first tried to worship me! I quickly put an end

---

[37] Acts 9:13-15

to that! I told him that I was an ordinary human being like he was! When I convinced him of that, he turned and introduced me to his family, his relatives and all his friends. The house was packed! He had invited them all over to hear me speak! This guy was an evangelist even before he became a believer. A few Christians could learn a lesson from him. He also told me about how God spoke to him in a dream, telling him that I was in Joppa and that he should send for me.

It was then that I finally understood God shows no partiality. My dream and Cornelius' were one. I laughed and began to share with them the gospel of Jesus Christ. I told them of all that Jesus did—how he died for our sins and was raised again so that we too might have new life.

God really has a sense of humor. God didn't even wait until I finished my sermon to send the Holy Spirit to move among those in Cornelius' home. What we disciples had experienced back in Jerusalem on Pentecost was now taking place even here among these Gentiles. Truly, God shows no partiality!

Later, when I shared with the other apostles back in Jerusalem what had happened, they too were excited and praised God for what God was now doing among those we once called barbarians.

But the devil wasn't going to give up. Herod began to seriously persecute us. He had James, John's brother, killed with a sword. Poor James! John was heartbroken. But Herod could not, would not, quiet that Son of Thunder with just a sword! Although he killed the man, the echo of his voice thunders on. Still, Herod saw how this pleased some of the Jews, and so he had me arrested. I guess he intended to do to me as he had done to James.

I suppose I'm a repeat offender. I confess it. This was my third time in prison. Twice by the temple authorities, and now by Herod himself! But after my last escape, Herod wasn't going to take any chances. I had to sleep with two guards chained to my side. There were guards at the door of my prison cell. And every six hours, four new guards took their place!

You might think I wouldn't sleep very well under such circumstances. But quite the opposite; I rested quite peacefully. I was beginning to get used to this place! Then, on my last night in prison, when I was sound asleep, I was startled by an angel whose presence lit my cell like it the mid-day sun! He told me to get up quickly and get ready to leave. I thought, "Hey, this is great, another dream! I wonder what God is going to tell me this time?" As I got up, the chains fell off my wrists. I put on my sandals and cloak and we began to walk out of the prison—past my cell door, past a guard who was oblivious to our presence, past a second guard, and out the front door! This was a neat dream!

When we reached the open air, I turned to the angel to find out what this dream was all about, but he was gone! I then realized this was no dream! It was real! After determining that it was probably not prudent to stand idle in front of the prison gate, I quickly left for the home of Mary, Mark's mother. Members of the church had often gathered there to pray, and so I figured that would be the best place to see some of the believers. I couldn't wait to tell them what had happened to me!

PETER

When I got to the door, I knocked. Finally, a servant by the name of Rhoda came to the door and asked who it was. I told her it was Peter. She was so excited and overjoyed she forgot to open the door and let me in! She ran back to the others, who were in the other room praying for my release, to tell them that I was just outside!

They thought she was out of her mind. I found this very funny. Here the church was praying for my release, but when it happened, they wouldn't believe it! She kept insisting it was me; they thought she was seeing things! Meanwhile, I'm stuck outside knocking on the door! They finally let me in and I was able to tell the story of my release. We all had a good laugh over that one!

The church continued to grow in some of the most unexpected places and among some of the most unlikely people. Even Saul of Tarsus, who we now know as Paul, became a believer! Who would have guessed that? He who persecuted the church with such vigor is now one of our most outspoken evangelists.

Like a pebble thrown into a pond, the gospel has continued to spread, just as Jesus said it would—first in Jerusalem, then Judea and Samaria, and then to the ends of the Earth. I guess that includes Indianola! *(Insert your home town...)*

Pentecost is indeed an amazing day in the life of Christ's church, for on that day, God poured out the Holy Spirit upon all who call upon his name. And that does not just include those of us who gathered in Jerusalem; it includes those of you who call yourselves by his name: *Christians*.

May that Spirit grant you God's peace. Shalom, both today and always. Shalom. That is a traditional Hebrew way of saying both hello and goodbye. It means "Greetings." It also means "Farewell." It means "God's blessings be upon you and your house." It means "Peace."

I want to teach you a traditional Hebrew folk-song. "Shalom chaverim, shalom chaverot, shalom, shalom." That is, "Peace, my dear friends. Le-hit-ra-ot, le-hit-ra-ot, shalom, shalom, until we meet again, peace."

(After singing it with congregation, Exit)

PETER

Discussion Questions: Petrine Part III

Which of the different vignettes shared from the book of Acts is your favorite? Why?

Do you see humor in some of Peter's stories? Does God have a sense of humor? How has God used humor to guide you in your faith?

The early church often suffered for its faith. Members were imprisoned, beaten, and even killed. But they often faced those persecutions with courage, even gratitude, that they should be counted worthy to suffer for the name of Christ. It is rare in our contemporary society that Christians face persecution to that degree, but is there a lesson here for us to grasp? What might that be?

Do you see a growing maturity in Peter as he shares with us his faith story in all three of these monologues? How have you grown in your journey with Christ?

MARY MAGDALENE

This may not technically be a monologue. As a man, it would be unrealistic for me to effectively play the role of a woman. Still, women played critical and essential roles in the biblical narrative, and they should never be overlooked! It was to women that Jesus first revealed his resurrected self. Mary Magdalene was the first evangelist.

I shared this story on an Easter morning with my congregation. Because I was inviting them into the mind of Mary, there was no costuming or staging.

My goal in this dialogue was to probe the inner mind of Mary. What was she feeling when she went to the tomb? How did her reactions change over the course of this wondrous story? From despair, grief, and fear to indescribable joy!

MARY MAGDALENE: *John 20:11-18*

WITH MARY IN THE GARDEN

When she found the tomb empty that morning, she ran back to tell Peter and John that someone took his body. Hearing the news, they hurried to the grave to see for themselves. Although she followed, she saw no point in chasing after them. Instead, she retraced her steps, for the second time this morning, to that horrible place. Not because she wanted to go...but because she had nowhere else she could go.

It was still dark, which was a good thing. Most people were still inside, either sound asleep or just beginning to stir. They didn't need to see her tears—her grief. She had to blink them away just to be able to see her path through the roughhewn stones to the garden.

Since that terrible day, she hadn't washed, brushed her hair, and, as a further sign of her mourning, she had put on her worst and grubbiest clothes. Those who could see would know immediately that she was deep in grief over the loss of someone dear to her. And how true that was!

She thought back over the last few years. Living in Magdala, on the western coast of the Sea of Galilee, it was not too surprising that their paths had crossed. Between his home in Nazareth and the community of Capernaum, to which he travelled often, he would have had to pass through her town frequently. Perhaps it was inevitable, even ordained, that they should meet.

Life before he showed up was a nightmare from which she could not wake. Despite the warm morning, she shivered at that memory. Back then, fear had dominated her life. And when she wasn't afraid, she was angry. Her emotions controlled her to such an extent that she found herself unable to function. Her family avoided her, leaving her even more lonely, frightened, and angry than ever.

How could her parents have known? As a child, they named her Mary. With a sad shake of her head, she acknowledged that she had lived up to her name's meaning: *bitter*. Life had been *bitter* to her and she became cynical, resentful, and, well, *bitter*.

But then, on one of his trips through Magdala, they met. He saw in her immediately what others either could not or would not see. He saw her fear and anger, but it did not frighten him or scare him away. Instead, he smiled, reached out to her, and said, "Mary!" Immediately, all the demons and terrors that consumed her for so long vanished. On his lips, her name was given new meaning. How can one voice contain so much power and so much tenderness? On his lips, Mary did not mean *bitter*...but *better*.

But now, he was gone and she felt the tug of those old emotions returning. She was lonely once again; he was gone. She was angry; how could they dare kill him and then justify it with pious words of defending the faith?! "Hypocrites!" She spat the word out with a vehemence that surprised even her.

But most of all, she was frightened: frightened that she would once again lose control of her life; frightened that she would return to the life she had before he came...frightened that she would never again experience the love and acceptance he showed to her.

She swallowed hard and shook her head. No; she would not go down that path again. She had been there once and knew it was a dead end. Yes, he may be gone, but he showed her there was another way—a better way. Perhaps her final gift to him would be to treasure and keep the precious gift of life he had given to her.

She continued her slow walk to the garden, to the tomb, and to a future that, at the moment, seemed as dark and as uncertain as the morning gloom. What would she do? Yes, during these last few years she had made some friends of those who walked with him. But with him gone, what would hold them together? Would they all return to their former lives and try to pick up where they left off?

Before she realized it, she arrived back in the garden. The olive trees, whose shade seemed so inviting during the heat of the day, looked more like ghostly specters in the early morning light. There was no welcome there.

It appeared that Peter and John already came, saw for themselves the final desecration of his body, and left, leaving her alone in the garden. At the sight of the tomb, the tears came once again, unbidden.

The need to look inside the tomb itself became overpowering—to see his final resting place, to perhaps even touch the very place where he once laid.

Bending over to look inside, she caught sight of two beings sitting on either end of the stone table where he once laid. Their presence startled her, for she thought she was alone in the garden. *"Woman, why are you weeping?"*[38] they asked. It was a seemingly ludicrous question in light of where they were sitting—in a tomb, among the dead—but without the one she was really looking for.

---

[38] John 20:13ff

"They have taken away my Lord, and I do not know where they have laid him." With those words, she voiced aloud what haunted her since that horrible Friday. *I don't know where he is...all I know is he isn't here with me.* With those words, she fled from the tomb, turning her back on the strangers and the awful emptiness that she felt.

In her hurry to escape from the tomb she nearly ran into someone else. He too could see her tears and asked, *"Woman, why are you weeping? Whom are you looking for?"* With a glimmer of hope, she thought that this gardener would certainly know where his body is. "Sir, if you have carried him away, tell me where you have laid him, and I will take him away."

"Mary!" There it was again—that one word spoken with both tremendous power and remarkable gentleness! That voice that can cut through the darkness and the gloom, the despair and the hopelessness! That voice that cannot be, and yet is! The bitterness in her mind once again vanished.

Rabbouni! Master! Only he could call her by name and draw her out of the pit of despair she dwelled in. He did in the garden what he did several years ago in Magdala: he lifted her out of fear, anger, and loneliness.

And so, once again, she found herself running to find the disciples, but this time with a very different attitude! The city, now stirring from its slumber, must have thought her an odd sight: someone dressed in the clothes of mourning but who was obviously overjoyed, running with an abandon that showed little respect for the dead she was supposed to be in mourning for. Perhaps they thought her crazy with grief, but she didn't care. All she knew was she now had the answer

109

MARY MAGDALENE: *John 20:11-18*

to the question that had haunted her: She no longer
needed to ask, where is he? She knew!

He is alive!

(Exit)

Discussion Questions: Mary Magdalene

Consider the four times Mary traversed the distance between Jerusalem, the disciples, and the garden tomb:

1. On her first walk to the tomb when she found the tomb empty;
2. as she hurried back to the disciples to tell them what she had found;
3. when she returned to the tomb alone after Peter and John had run ahead of her; and
4. on her final trip to the disciples with the news that she had seen the risen Jesus.

What might she have been feeling? How might she have been moving?

"Mary!" With the simple call of her name, Jesus identifies himself to her. Mary's name means "bitter," but in the mouth of Jesus, that takes on a new reality. How would hearing your name on the lips of Jesus affect you?

At first, Mary did not recognize Jesus, supposing him to be the gardener. When we see someone out of context, in a place we do not expect to see them, we sometimes fail to recognize them. Are there times we fail to see Jesus in our world today because he is in a place we wouldn't expect him to be?

ANANIAS

One of the reasons I chose to portray this character was because I was interested in exploring a lesser known individual in Scripture who nonetheless had an immense effect on the Christian narrative. In this sense, Ananias is like the Minor Prophets in the Old Testament. They are called minor not because they are of less importance but because of the smaller size of their books compared to those of some of the other prophets. Ananias is a minor character in the book of Acts not because he is less important than Paul, Peter, or Luke but because we know less about him in the narrative.

Because we have less narrative to work with, I faced some interesting challenges as I sought to imagine his life and his reaction to being called by God to reach out to Saul.

I chose to portray Ananias later in his life, reflecting over how God called him to minister to Saul. As Ananias enters, he refers to a local celebrity. You, obviously, would have to select someone that your congregation would know.

Because of Ananias' faithfulness, we have the apostle Paul who played such a significant role in the early church and who wrote so many of the letters in our New Testament. Oh, surely God would have found someone else, but it was Ananias who said, "Yes," although I have to believe even he had his share of doubts about what God was asking him to do.

ANANIAS

(Ananias enters, stooped, with a cane, and chuckling to himself.)

Yes, we all do this, and yes I've heard some of you do it too! Oh, how we like to make ourselves sound important by naming famous people that we knew before they were famous. Somehow, I guess, that makes us seem a little more important—a little more famous ourselves! I know some of you knew Casey Blake, senator so and so, or some other celebrity before their name meant anything to the rest of the world.

Well, I too knew someone before he became famous. I knew him before he became known by his more popular name. I knew him when he was still called Saul. In fact, by the grace of God, I had a role in making him famous!

So who am I? My name is Ananias. But please don't confuse me with two others who go by that same name. Neither are remembered fondly. One was killed by the Holy Spirit for lying and withholding gifts to the church. Another Ananias was a high priest who had no interest in the growth of the church.

Me? I'm just a simple disciple who has lived his entire life in Damascus. Let me share with you how I met this "Saul" character. One day, I was in the middle of my devotional time, praying and meditating. Nothing special about that; I'm sure many of you do the same! But in the middle of this time, I was interrupted by God!

God called me by name, *"Ananias!"* And like a good disciple, I responded, "Here I am Lord." But what

God had to say next just about turned my answer from, "Here I am," to, "There I go!" I desperately wanted to pull a Jonah. You'll remember, Jonah was told to go to Nineveh, so he high tailed it in the opposite direction. I definitely could sympathize with that prophet!

God told me to search out and find a man by the name of Saul who was from Tarsus. God said that he had spoken to Saul and told him to expect me! (Somehow that seemed a little presumptuous of God. Shouldn't God have asked me first to see if my calendar was open?) Anyway, God told me I should lay my hands upon Saul and heal his blindness.

This truly frightened me because I had heard stories about this man, Saul. He had recently received extradition papers from the religious leaders in Jerusalem to come to Damascus and arrest those who claimed to be followers of Jesus and then to transport them back to Jerusalem for trial. I told God this very thing! "Besides, Lord," I said, "he may be using this as a ruse, a form of entrapment, to catch us! His feigned blindness might be the cheese and I could be the mouse!"

But God only repeated his command to me: *"Go, for this man will be an instrument to bring my name before Gentiles and kings and before the people of Israel. I myself will show him how much he must suffer for the sake of my name."*[39]

An instrument, huh? I wonder what kind of an instrument he will be. An axe to cut us down? A spear to impale us? A hammer to beat us into submission? Still, I was convinced that it was God who had spoken

---

[39] Acts 9:15-16

to me, so with fear and trembling, I went. God even provided me with directions. I guess that shouldn't have surprised me. God knows our address. God knows where we are all the time. In this case, Saul was staying on the street called Straight at the house of Judas. I knew the place and had passed by it often. And so, with much trepidation, I left.

All too soon I arrived at the house and was ushered into the room where Saul was staying. I found him kneeling on the floor in prayer. He was truly blind and weak with hunger, for he had not eaten or had anything to drink for the past three days. He certainly did not seem to be the terrible threat I had heard he was.

For a moment, I paused, uncertain about where to begin, or what to do. Hearing me enter, he turned his head my way, as if trying to ascertain who was in the room with him. What was I to do? I knelt by him and introduced myself as Ananias, a follower of Jesus Christ. Looking to me, without seeing, tears were flooding his eyes. In his face shown regret, confusion, joy, and anticipation all mixed together in a puzzling synthesis that threatened to overwhelm him emotionally.

I asked him what had happened, and he explained. Some of it I had already heard—that he truly had come from Jerusalem prepared to arrest those who professed that Jesus was the Messiah. But on the way, something quite miraculous had happened. While on the road, he was confronted by the very person whose followers he was seeking to destroy. In a flash of light that knocked him to his knees, he heard the voice of Jesus asking why he was persecuting Him. Then Jesus told him to finish his trip to Damascus and once he got there, he would be told what to do. But he discovered, when he tried to stand up, he could no longer see. His travelling companions had to lead him the rest of the way by hand in order for him to get to the city.

I was amazed at his story. It was a good thing that he couldn't see my face; I smiled because I noticed that God had told me more about his future than God had even told him! If I had told him then that he was to a prophet to the Gentiles and to kings and to the people of Israel and that God was going to reveal to him how much he was to suffer for God's name, he might have gone running out into the streets! One thing was for sure, if God hadn't yet told him, I certainly wasn't going to either! In a further irony, this man who had caused so much suffering for those who professed Jesus was now going to suffer himself on account of that name!

I was deeply touched by his story and realized that this man was not the enemy I thought he was. The next words threatened to get caught in my throat as I spoke them. I placed my hands on him and said, "Brother Saul, the Lord Jesus, who appeared to you on your way here, has sent me so that you may regain your sight and be filled with the Holy Spirit."[40]

Immediately, something fell from his eyes and he could once again see. He was baptized into the faith, and together we ate and drank. He began to ask me all sorts of questions about Jesus, many that I could not even begin to answer. I was amazed at the depth and perceptiveness of his questions and the intense hunger he had to learn more.

---

[40] Acts 8:17

Well, you know the rest of his story. You have read about his missionary journeys, his stories as recorded in Scripture, and, most well-known, his many letters that he has written to the churches. He certainly did preach to the Gentiles...and even to kings.

It's kind of ironic that it was on a street named Straight that this man made a major U-turn in his life. Yet, this man who I thought an enemy has been made a brother through and in Christ.

(Exit)

Discussion Questions: Ananias

God knows our address. Is that a comforting or disturbing idea?

What do you think happened to Ananias that he could change from calling Saul "this man who has done much evil to the saints" to "brother"? Are there people in our lives whom we need to call "sister/brother"?

Ananias is one of the minor characters in the New Testament. He is only mentioned in this passage in Acts and then he disappears into history. And yet the effect he had on one of the greatest saints in Christendom is profound. Most of us will never show up in a book of Christian history. Reflect on the idea of faithfulness and anonymity. While we may be an unknown to most of humanity, we are known by God.

PAUL IN PRISON

Paul is such a fascinating character, and his epistles and the book of Acts contain many wonderful stories that could become the basis for a monologue. I could have chosen Paul with Silas in the Philippian prison, or the story of his ride in a ship and subsequent wreck on his way to Rome. For this monologue however, I chose his time under house arrest while in Rome. Scholars generally agree that he wrote several of his letters (Philippians, Colossians, Philemon and perhaps Ephesians) during this time. His letter to the church in Philippi becomes the basis for a dialogue in this portrayal. Although scholars debate the Pauline authorship of Ephesians, I have chosen to refer to a part of that epistle in this story.

In his book, *Paul: Apostle of the Heart Set Free,* F. F. Bruce relates the book of Acts to Paul's epistles. I wanted to help connect those two in this monologue. I also wanted to express Paul's deep love of Christ and his passion for the church. I want the congregation to understand that deep Christian joy is not dependent upon outward circumstances. The book of Philippians—a book full of joy—was written in what many of us would call a dark time!

The staging is a simple desk and stool, a collection of scrolls on the desk and on a primitive shelf behind the desk, feather quills to be used as writing instruments, and some kind of ink well. A plate of apples sits on the desk. To show that he is under house arrest, Paul is, quite literally, chained to the desk. The chain is long enough to allow him to enter and exit the stage and to move freely. Because this story is set

121

PAUL

toward the end of Paul's life, I have chosen to portray him as an older man, bent over, but no less bubbling with energy and passion.

*Some of the inspiration from this particular monologue comes from the powerful presentation by Dean Jones, titled *St. John in Exile*. I deeply commend that to you for your viewing.

A VISIT WITH PAUL

(Paul enters, reading a scroll and eating an apple.) "Finally, my friends, whatever is true, whatever is honorable, whatever is just, whatever is pure, whatever is pleasing" *(He bites into the apple)*...hmmm, "whatever is tasty," no, no, "whatever is commendable, if there is any excellence and if there is anything worthy of praise, think about these things."[41]

Oh, visitors! Shalom, my friends. Welcome! It's great to have you here in my humble dwelling. Can I offer you something to eat? Perhaps something to drink? These apples are delicious. Some friends from the Roman church dropped them off just a little while ago. Are you sure? Well, suit yourself. *(He takes another bite.)* Oh, this? *(He raises a portion of the chain.)* Well, as you can see, I'm under house arrest, awaiting trial for confessing Christ. I'm under constant guard.

Well, not under *constant* guard. (*He looks both ways conspiratorially.)* Shhh, Claudius had to step out for a few moments. Even soldiers of the Roman cohort have to answer to a higher authority than Caesar, and no, I am not referring to God...at least not directly. So please, don't tell anybody that Claudius has briefly left his post. I would hate to get him into trouble. Besides, I'm hardly a flight risk. *(He gestures to the chain.)*

I've got high hopes for Claudius. After all, guarding me can't be the most exciting of assignments. Watching an old man write and receive letters and greet the occasional visitor must seem pretty boring to a young

---

[41] Philippians 4:8

man. Why, just yesterday, in one of his more bored moments, he asked me why I spend all my time writing. *(He gestures to table with a sly wink and chuckle.)* "Oh, just writing to some friends of mine in Philippi," I told him. "Oh, really?" he says. "What are you saying to them?" *(He chuckles again.)* Well, I tell you. I just couldn't let that go by; it was just too big of an opening. Although I'm the prisoner here, I think he was the captive audience!

As we talked, I even taught him one of our Christian songs, which I included in my letter. *(He gestures to the letter.)* You know the one. It's that great song about our Lord.

> who, though he was in the form of God,
> did not regard equality with God
> as something to be exploited,
> but emptied himself,
> taking the form of a slave,
> being born in human likeness.
> And being found in human form,
> he humbled himself
> and became obedient to the point of death—
> even death on a cross.
> Therefore God also highly exalted him
> and gave him the name
> that is above every name,
> so that at the name of Jesus
> every knee should bend,
> in heaven and on earth and under the earth,
> and every tongue should confess
> that Jesus Christ is Lord,

to the glory of God the Father.[42]

How I love those words! I never tire of hearing them!
Poor Claudius. He just didn't quite know what to make
of it. God becoming a man was nothing new to him. It
happens all the time in their pagan legends of Zeus and
the other false gods. But this God-man is different.
Claudius couldn't get over the idea that this God-man
died for people! Not only that, but he came back to life!
He was resurrected and glorified! And eventually
everyone—Jews and Romans, slaves and the nobility,
those in chains *(He gestures to chains)* and those who
are free—shall kneel and confess Jesus Christ as Lord.
As you can imagine, Claudius had lots of questions.

And, would you believe it, Claudius even helped me
write one of my own letters! I was writing to the
Ephesians and I was looking for a way to tell them how
to defend themselves against the ways of the devil.
Claudius was just standing there, minding his own
business, resplendent in his battle dress. And then it hit
me! Of course! To defend oneself against the devil you
must use: the belt of truth; the breastplate of
righteousness; the shoes, the gospel of peace. You must
have the shield of faith and the helmet of salvation. I
had Claudius show me each piece and describe how he
put it on and what it was used for. And as he talked, I
wrote it all down. But it was he who told me that a
Roman soldier without a sword would be out of
uniform. A sword! How could I have forgotten the
sword? The sword shall be...the word of God! With it,

---

[42] Philippians 2:6-11

we shall take God's Kingdom into the world and defeat the plans of the devil.[43]

Keep praying for Claudius. He's close—this close *(He gestures with his fingers)*—to professing Christ. I'm guessing he will become a believer before I send this off. *(He motions to his letter.)* Then he can join the other guards who have confessed Christ because they were chained to me!

(He gives a hearty laugh.) Isn't God's sense of humor great? To keep me from preaching about Jesus Christ, I'm arrested. And while I'm awaiting trial, I have already converted a growing number of Caesar's own guards! There's Antony, Marcus, Philonius, and the others. Soon, by the grace and mercy of God, Claudius will join them. If the trial doesn't happen soon, they may have to release me because I'm a bigger liability to them under house arrest than I was as a free man! *(He laughs again.)* And on top of that, I also have the time now to write to all these churches *(he gestures to other scrolls)* that I love so dearly. For me, it's a win-win situation. So what does it matter if I am free or under arrest? Christ is nonetheless proclaimed in every way, and in this I rejoice![44]

But don't get me wrong, my friends. I do so desperately wish to visit the churches again and see how they are faring. *(With eagerness, he says,)* Tell me, do you carry any news from those churches? Perhaps of Corinth, Thessalonica, or Antioch? Perhaps even of Jerusalem? Are the believers there remaining steadfast and faithful? Are they growing in the Lord? *(He is*

---

[43] See Ephesians 6:10-17
[44] Philippians 1:18

disappointed.) No news? *(He sighs.)* I pray for those churches daily. Many of them are so small and young in their faith. They are easy and tempting pickings for those who have distorted the truth of God for their own ends.

There are those who claim that in order to be faithful followers of Jesus, Gentile converts must first become Jews before becoming Christians. They claim our Gentile brothers and sisters must follow all the legalistic codes that burden and entrap people. No! *(He stamps his fist on the desk.)* It is from that very kind of bondage that Christ has set us free!

Some believers have gone to the other extreme. Having been forgiven and freed by the blood of Christ, they think they can do anything! These have slipped into some of the most degrading and immoral practices. It has become so bad that even those outside the church are shocked by their actions! This is not what God has in mind for us.

Then there are others who have become enticed by silly philosophies and pointless discussions that have little relevance to our lives. They only serve to distract us from pursuing a deeper relationship with God.

And so, not being able to be physically present with them, I write—and write, and write—to the Philippians, to the Ephesians, to those in Colossae! *(He gestures again to letters on the shelf.)* And good and faithful friends just like you who are headed that way deliver them for me. Now that I've mentioned it, which way are you heading? Perhaps, if you are able to wait a day or two, you could carry a letter for me?

What's that? You had a question? What's it like to be the famous apostle to the Gentiles? *(He pauses.)*

Many would argue just the opposite. To them, I am the infamous apostle. *(He reflects.)* What's it like?

My friends, it would be very easy to boast. And believe me, if I wanted to, I could brag at great length! As a good Jew, I was circumcised on the eighth day: a member of the people of Israel, of the tribe of Benjamin, a Hebrew born of Hebrews; as to the law, a Pharisee; as to zeal, a persecutor of the church; as to righteousness under the law, blameless. But...and I can't say this strong enough: I count them all as garbage—no, I need an even stronger word. I count them as...*sewage*—yes *sewage!*—in comparison to knowing Christ and the power of his resurrection.[45]

Say, that's pretty good! Excuse me while I write that down! *(He writes on a piece of scrap parchment.)* I count them all as...what did I say? Oh, God, help me remember! As, as *sewage* in comparison to knowing Christ and the power of his resurrection. There. Maybe I'll have to incorporate that into my letter somewhere.

So some think of me as the famous Paul, evangelist to the Gentiles and great expositor of the gospel. *(He shakes his head.)* If only you knew. You think God chose me because of a great scholarly mind or a physical condition that allows me to travel? Or that he chose me for my temperament that borders on impudence that allows me the courage to preach in some of the most outrageous of places? Hardly. God chose this thickheaded, stubborn, and rebellious hypocrite, and persecutor of the church to reveal the depth and magnitude of God's grace and mercy. If God

---

[45] Philippians 3:5-10 – my paraphrase

can forgive and change me, then God can forgive and change anybody!

It never ceases to amaze me that God has chosen me. I have told the story so many times over the years as I have visited different churches and written countless letters. I think I tell the story, as much for myself as for others, to convince and remind us both of the depth of God's mercy and love.

There was a time, my friends, when I was walking a very different path. I was convinced that these followers of this "Jesus" were a serious threat to my Jewish faith. I believed it was my sacred duty to rout them out—to purge the faith of my ancestors of this heresy. I became its most outspoken opponent! I argued against them in the synagogues. I witnessed against them in the courts. I even assisted in their deaths! Even my own teacher, the blessed Gamaliel, thought I had gone a bit too far!

But in truth, I believed I hadn't yet gone far enough! I sought to chase them down wherever they might be, even in far off Damascus!

It happened when I was just a few miles outside of that city: a light so blinding it knocked me off my horse and onto my knees. *(He falls to his knees.)* It was then that I heard a voice saying, *"Saul, Saul, why do you persecute me?" (He shades his eyes and looks up.)* Blinded and confused, I called back, "Who are you, Lord?" The voice responded, *"I am Jesus, whom you are persecuting. Now get up and go into the city, for I have work for you to do."*[46]

---

[46] Acts 9:4-7

(He gets off of his knees, with difficulty.) Well, how does one argue with a voice from heaven? For the first, and some might say only time, in my life, I was at a loss for words. I had been wrong...majorly wrong. But I vowed then to change my ways and obey that voice. For all my faults, and I have many, I can't stand being wrong. If I had to study and pray for the rest of my life to learn God's truth, I would. And by the grace of God, I have done both, and I have done both often.

Don't get the impression that God is done with me yet. I'm far from where God wants me to be. I've got so much still to learn. *(He numbers them off.)* Right now I'm re-reading the prophet Isaiah. I'm discussing with friends the life of Abraham. Well, there is so much I still want to understand. It's like...like...it's like a runner stretching to reach the finish line *(he pulls his chain to its limit)* straining forward to the goal. Like that runner, I am pressing onward toward the prize of the heavenly call of God in Christ Jesus.[47]

Perseverance: that's what it's all about. It's about allowing no hurdle or obstacle to interfere with your service and discipleship. You want an example of perseverance? Let me tell you about Epaphroditus. Like you, he came to visit me in my chains. He came from the church in Philippi with news of the church and gifts from the believers there.

But the trip almost killed him. When I saw him, he was very sick. It took him a long time for him to recover. But here's the amazing surprise. Even while he was on what we thought was his deathbed, his friends back in Philippi sent me news of their concern for his

---

[47] Philippians 3:14

welfare. And then, this great saint of God was distressed because he discovered that his friends back in Philippi were worried about him! He was worried about them because they were worrying about him! *(He shakes his head in disbelief.)*

But in God's mercy, Epaphroditus recovered, and I'm sending him back to his friends in Philippi with this letter, if I can ever finish it!

Serving God may be a rewarding task, but no one has ever said that it would be easy. Epaphroditus is a good example of that. Hmmmm, what's that? And so are my chains? *(He chuckles.)* I suppose so. But these *(he lifts his chains)* are nothing compared to some other things I've gone through. For example, I've been whipped four times. Or was it five? I keep losing count. I was beaten with rods on three other occasions. Once, in Galatia, I was stoned and left for dead. I've been shipwrecked three times, and on one of those I was drifting in the sea for 24 hours! And then there are the dangers of just traveling from town to town—dangers in the form of thieves, animals, the weather...[48]

Oh dear, there I go again, sounding like I'm bragging about all I've been through. That couldn't be further from the truth. I'm just trying to show you how God can give you the strength—yes, even the *joy*—in the middle of the most trying of circumstances. I guess what I'm trying to say is that my intent is not just to share with you my biography—what a boring thing that would be—but rather a theography. I am trying to tell not just my story but God's story in my life.

---

[48] See 2 Corinthians 11:24-27

PAUL

Excuse me, but I just have to finish this letter. Thank you so much for coming and spending this time with me. Your presence has brightened my day, lightened my load, and inspired my work. *(He raises his hand in blessing.)* May the grace of our Lord Jesus Christ be with you. Now if you will please excuse me, I must get back to my writing.

(He picks up his quill and sits down.) What word do my Philippian friends need to hear? Like me, they too are struggling with trials and difficulties. Yes! That's it exactly! *(He writes and says,)* "Rejoice in the Lord always, my friends, again I say, rejoice! Let your gentleness be known to everyone. The Lord is near. Do not worry about anything, but in everything by prayer and supplication with thanksgiving let your requests be made know to God. And the peace of God, which surpasses all understanding will guard your hearts and your minds in Christ Jesus."[49]

(He looks off stage.) It looks like Claudius is coming back. Oh, Claudius. *(Exiting, he takes a bowl of fruit.)* Good to see you back. How about an apple? This reminds me about something I wrote a few years back about the fruit of the Spirit...

---

[49] Philippians 4:4-7

Discussion Questions: Paul in Prison

Reread the book of Philippians, keeping in mind that Paul wrote this letter while in prison to a small church that was struggling with persecution. How was Paul's own life an example? What words did he share to inspire them? What does that say to us today?

Imagine that on one of his many journeys Paul visited your church. He knows you and your people. Then, perhaps a year later, Paul writes a letter to your church. What are some of the things he might say? Where would he praise you in your ministry? Where might he give encouragement or correction?

In the monologue, Paul shares the story of Epaphroditus and uses him as an example of faithfulness and perseverance. Who in your life would you name?

Several times in the book of Acts, and also in the epistles, Paul tells his story of meeting Jesus on the road to Damascus. Every believer has a story of meeting with Jesus. Some are dramatic; others may seem more modest in comparison, but all are valid. Can you share your story?

JOHN KNOX

The Scottish reformer John Knox (c.1514-1572) is obviously not a name that shows up in our Bibles, and as such doesn't quite belong in this collection of monologues taken from the biblical narrative. Therefore, you can consider the inclusion of this monologue as an appendix to the project that precedes it. He appears much more recently in church history. He would be the first to argue stridently against putting himself and his words on an equal par with Scripture. My insertion of this monologue at the end of this book is in no way intended to suggest that his message should be weighed equally with Scripture.

Nevertheless, God has used, and will continue to use, women and men to speak and articulate God's Word to their times and cultures. Along with John Calvin and countless others, John Knox stands as one of those individuals whom God has used to help shape and form my Presbyterian heritage.

The stewardship committee of my church suggested, or should I say *challenged* me, on the 500th anniversary of John Knox's birthday to prepare a stewardship monologue in which I play the role of the Scottish reformer. I accepted the challenge.

The monologue that follows shares his story. John Knox was one of the key contributors to what later became known as the Scots Confession, and I have also utilized and quoted from that confession.

As a student of church history, I find the Protestant Reformation in the British Isles very frustrating. It seemed they just couldn't make up their minds: Catholic, Protestant, Catholic, and then Protestant

135

again. The English and the Scots were often in disagreement, and to make matters worse, it seemed that just about everyone was named Mary, Elizabeth or John!

Expecting that I wasn't the only one with this difficulty, I prepared my staging accordingly. Using pictures I found online, I color-printed the faces of six people John Knox interacted with during his life: George Wishart, Mary Tudor, John Calvin, Mary of Guise, Mary Stewart, and Queen Elizabeth. I attached these to twelve-inch paint sticks and planted them in six large pots, which were strategically located on stage. As I told Knox's story, I interacted with the appropriate face.

Center stage sat a desk with writing utensils and a pen. My costume consisted of a black robe, sandals, a Scottish tam and a grey beard.

I feigned a Scottish accent for the first paragraph of the monologue, but upon recognizing the audience, I aided them by losing the accent. This was done both for their sakes and mine, as I doubted I could sustain a believable Scottish accent for the entire monologue.

John Knox's fiery and prophetic voice paved the way for the Scottish reformation and for what ultimately took root in America as the Presbyterian Church. But he was also a man of his age, culture, and human fallibility. His strong anti-Catholic beliefs and his infamous stand against women in leadership are hard for us to hear today. Historically, we may understand why he held those beliefs, even if we do not agree. Nevertheless, we are grateful to God for his remarkable story and his contribution to our heritage.

A VISIT WITH JOHN KNOX

(John is sitting at the desk, writing and reading aloud.) August 17, in the year of our Lord, fifteen hundred sixty. Long have we thirsted, dear brethren, to make known to the world the sum of that doctrine which we profess and for which we have sustained infamy and danger. But such has been the rage of Satan against us, and against Jesus Christ's eternal truth, lately born again among us that to this day no time has been granted us to clear our consciences, as most gladly we would have done.[50]

Rage: aye, that's the truth of it! For nearly twenty years now I have fought, scratched, pleaded, argued, and debated in and for the name of our Lord. My weapons have been the pen and the sword and my travelling bag. For my efforts I have been maligned, arrested, imprisoned, and enslaved. But perhaps now, finally, by the grace of God, the kirk in my beloved Scotland will be free to worship as Scripture commands us.

Ei, but my path has been one full of turns and surprises! In my early ignorance, I was ordained to the very church against which I have struggled against these many years. But our Lord drew me to himself and I saw the truth of it when I was about twenty-nine years of age. It wasn't long after that I met George Wishart. *(He moves to the picture of George Wishart.)* Ne're a man of God like him!

He always seemed to be one step ahead of the authorities who sought to have him arrested as he went

---

[50] Knox, John, Preface to the Scots Confession.

from town to town preaching. I often stood with him, even holding a sword to protect him! But when he knew he truly was about to be arrested, he sent me on my way, saying, "One is sufficient for a sacrifice."

His arrest and martyrdom galvanized the people. The castle in St. Andrews was stormed, and that phony and heretical popinjay, Bishop Beaton, was killed. Much to my surprise, I was asked to come to the castle and serve as the chaplain for those who had taken refuge there. Alas, the French were asked to come, and they laid siege to the castle, eventually taking it. For nineteen horrific months, I was shackled to an oar on a French galley, starving and near death.

But God is good, and through the intervention of the English court, I was released, and for a few years I served as a pastor in both Berwick and London. *(He moves to the picture of Mary Tudor.)* But when that wicked English Jezebel, Mary Tudor, became ruler in fifteen hundred and fifty-three, there was little tolerance for truth.

During her five-year reign as Catholic monarch over England, many Protestant reformers were imprisoned, killed, or forced to flee to Europe. Over 280 were burned at the stake, thus giving her the name "bloody Mary." Hundreds of others left the country. I was one of those who had to go into hiding, and eventually I fled to France, and from there to Geneva.

Geneva! This remarkable city must be the closest thing to God's Kingdom here on earth! God has used their pastor and teacher, John Calvin, in mighty ways! *(He moves to John Calvin.)* Oh, he was a bit too reserved and scholarly for my taste, and I suspect in his eyes I was too brash and fiery! But the things I learned while I was there, aye! I committed to paper and memory so much that I wanted to bring back to the kirk in Scotland.

Although I definitely didn't get along with Mary Tudor, *(he points to her)* I had greater hope for Mary of Guise *(he moves to Mary Guise),* who was the queen regent in my homeland. She seemed to be more tolerant of Protestants, even if she did continue in her Catholic ways. When I tried to convince her to become a Protestant, she laughed at me and called me a joke. From then on, things only went from bad to worse.

I confess that I have had a real problem over the years with women in roles of leadership. Mary Tudor, Mary of Guise as regent in Scotland, Elizabeth, and later Mary Stewart. Perhaps God put them there to test me! Remember that brash side of me? Well, I once wrote a treatise titled, "The First Blast of the Trumpet Against the Monstrous Regiment of Women." Ostensibly, I was writing specifically against the evils of Mary Tudor, but just as it was being published, Mary Tudor died and her half-sister Elizabeth took her place. *(He moves to Elizabeth.)* Bad timing! As you can imagine, the new Queen Elizabeth didn't take it too kindly. She had supported my work, and I offended her! Later, I modified my views to those that were less provocative, and she was mollified.

Eventually, I was able to return to my beloved homeland, and although there were many struggles yet to be had, progress was being made. When Mary of Guise died in 1560, the French withdrew permanently from Scotland and agreed not to interfere. Nevertheless, her daughter, Mary Queen of the Scots *(he moves to Mary Stewart),* assumed her role as the new ruler. Like her mother, she respected the Protestant faith but would not turn from her own Catholic traditions. Despite five different meetings with her, some of which were very heated, I could not persuade her otherwise.

But because of her tolerance, the time was ripe for the Scottish parliament to act, and I pushed hard for them to adopt a confession of faith that would guide the kirk in the reformed tradition. Six of us gathered together to write this confession. By God's grace, it took us only four days! Well, there was John Douglas, John Hillock, John Rowe, John Winram, and John Spottiswoode, and, of course, me-John! As you can see, our passion for the Scottish kirk was not the only thing we shared in common!

On this, the five hundredth year of my birthday— which might explain the beard—what can I share with you? What gift do I have for you? We in the Scottish kirk believe that the true kirk only exists when three things are present: the word of God rightly preached, the correct administration of the sacraments—namely the Lord's Supper and baptism—and, perhaps surprisingly for some of you, the third is ecclesiastical discipline in order to repress vice and nourish virtue. Where these three things exist, the true kirk of Jesus Christ is present.[51]

Let me put it this way, in the words that my friends and I penned in the opening paragraph of that confession the Scottish parliament overwhelmingly adopted on that great day in August of 1560. These are the words that we have so longingly wished to profess to the world but until that moment were restrained to do

---

[51] Scots Confession, Article 18.

so by Satan's rage. These are the words that give voice
to our faith:

> We confess and acknowledge one God alone, to
> whom we alone must cleave, whom alone we
> must serve, whom only we must worship, and in
> whom alone we put our trust. Who is eternal,
> infinite, immeasurable, incomprehensible,
> omnipotent, invisible; one in substance and yet
> distinct in three persons, the Father, the Son and
> the Holy Ghost. By whom we confess and
> believe all things in heaven and earth, visible
> and invisible, to have been created, to be
> retained in their being, and to be ruled and
> guided by God's inscrutable providence for such
> end as God's eternal wisdom, goodness, and
> justice have appointed, and to the manifestation
> of God's own glory.

On this, your stewardship Sunday, I urge you to hear
these words. It is to God alone we must cleave. It is
God alone we must serve. It is God alone we must
worship. It is in God alone that we place our trust. What
is stewardship but a recognition of these very things?

Some might think I was tough and argumentative
only with those in positions of authority. In fairness, I
never minced my words, regardless of who I was
talking to. A couple of years before we drafted this
confession, I wrote an open letter to the Scottish people.
I challenged those who thought that because they were
not wealthy or influential or of royal blood that their
role in faith was inconsequential. Where did I put that
scrap? Ah, here it is! *(He rummages around on desk for
scrap of paper, finds it, and reads from i.t)*

141

JOHN KNOX (*1513-1572*)

> Neither would I that you should esteem the reformation and care of religion less to appertain to you, because you are not kings, rulers, judges, nobles, nor in authority. Beloved brethren, you are God's creatures, created and formed to his own image and similitude, for whose redemption was shed the most precious blood of the only beloved Son of God.[52]

I would venture that not many of you are kings, rulers, judges, nobles, or people in great authority. But you are God's creatures, created in God's image. And it was Jesus Christ who shed his blood for you.

It is this eternal, infinite, immeasurable, incomprehensible, omnipotent, and invisible God whom we worship. Let us do so with all that we are. That is stewardship.

(Exit)

---

[52] John Knox, *Exhortation to the Commonality of Scotland*, 1558, Found in *Writings of John Knox* (London, England: Religious Tract Society, 1831), 222.

Discussion Questions: John Knox

One of the values of studying church history is that it helps us keep our place in the long story we know as the church in perspective. John Knox was a man of his time. In retrospect, we struggle with some of his biases. And yet, God did a mighty work through him. 500 years from now, our spiritual ancestors may shake their heads at our biases. Nevertheless, how may God be using the church today in mighty ways?

John Knox said there were three things that marked the true church of Jesus Christ. What were they? Do you agree? One of them is probably a bit surprising. Did it make better sense in his time than it does in our own?

John Knox's faith was shaped by many people. There were those who encouraged and supported him— George Wishart and John Calvin—and others whose opposition helped him to define his beliefs. Who in your life has helped, or is helping, to form your faith?

AUTHOR BIOGRAPHY

 Rev. David Endriss has been a pastor for nearly 30 years serving Presbyterian congregations in Alaska, Minnesota and Iowa. The amazing stories of Scripture have often captivated his imagination.

David is married to Nicola, whom he met in England when attending a Bible School in Great Britain. They have two sons: Paul and Robert. They also have four grand-children whom they adore.

David enjoys travelling, hiking, art history, and reading science fiction and historical mysteries.

19547726R00088

Printed in Great Britain
by Amazon